Trailblazer

Finding the Path - Showing the Way

By Paul C. Buechel, M.D.

Trailblazer

Finding the Path – Showing the Way

Paul C. Buechel, M.D.

Fitting Words

Published by Fitting Words LLC

Also by Paul C. Buechel, M.D.
Available wherever books are sold.

Dedication

This volume is dedicated to, first and foremost, God our heavenly Father and our Lord and Savior Jesus the Christ, as well as to the kingdom work they ask every one of us to step into and perform.

I dedicate *Trailblazer* to the reader as well. May we be persistently open to hearing the divine voice, be consistently trying to understand God's plan for our journey ahead, and be always willing to follow his commands.

I also dedicate this to my dear and supportive wife, Victoria, and my amazing daughter, Lexie, as well as the rest of my family, my friends, and all who have contributed to this subject matter through example, discussion, or involvement in my sometimes crazy adventures.

I additionally must give great credit and thanks to my excellent publisher, Dan Wright of Fitting Words, and my brilliant editor, Thom Chittom. Their assistance is priceless.

My prayer for *Trailblazer* is that our Lord God will use this work he has inspired for whatever means he has intended as his Spirit spreads his saving good news over our globe!

Table of Contents

Introduction

Trailblazer. Be the first. Be a leader. Be the one who absolutely and positively changes your family, your group of friends, your school, your team, or your workplace!

We all have a life compass, that is, a primary focus. It colors and affects our entire life's journey, our expedition through this world. It is a pathfinder guiding us through our wildernesses and over our un-blazed trails.

Our impassible forests teach us that we cannot do this journey alone. When out in the wilds, we come to realize how truly dependent we are upon God, and our complacency quickly disappears.

***

Being in the woods and wilderness far from any sign of humanity deeply stirs my heart and soul. Yet, I understand that not many people share this perception. Most are more comfortable in domesticated home environments, tucked snugly within their fancy cities and suburbs.

While such is certainly fine and a sign of our times, I believe we must sometimes get into the wilderness, physically as well as metaphorically. We require wildernesses in our lives. What if everything was perfect all the time? We would have no need of help or fellowship from our Lord or from others. Each would simply be living in his own little bubble of a seemingly perfect world, doing exactly what he wants and having exactly what he always desires.

I propose that instead of always painstakingly striving to get out of the wilderness via our own power as soon as we can, let's consider embracing it instead! In this past century in particular, modern society has advanced out of its physical wilderness. Many people never get out into deep woods anymore. Now, we spend more time in abstract and metaphorical dilemmas and events. Our environments are proper and controlled, temperature is regulated, and elements are sanitized. We are not exposed to biting insects, wild beasts, and other physical challenges and discomforts. We never give them a thought.

However, since the world's post-Eden era began, such hardships have been part of every human experience. And I believe that those challenges brought people closer to God.

Natives I meet in Africa who still exist in the difficult conditions their tribes have endured for centuries seem to have a closer perception of fellowship with God. They realize how much they rely on him daily for their needs. Our wildernesses do that for us.

When we reduce our wilderness exposure, removing its insects and elements from our lives, we perceive a false self-reliance. We feel independent. We rationalize that we don't really need God's help—unless we get into dire straits.

In the wilderness, there are quicksand pits and bear traps, the dangers of becoming hypothermic or directionally disoriented or sustaining a fractured limb in a fall off a cliff. The challenges in our modern wildernesses are more veiled or camouflaged. We strive to protect ourselves from their harsh realities, and in so doing, we insulate ourselves from our Creator father as well.

We forget that it is not our sanitized environments but God who takes care of us. There is great freedom in this realization. The wilderness makes it obvious that we cannot do this journey alone. That is God's message for us. This was the message he impressed upon his nation in their wilderness after delivery from Egypt, and it is the message he desires us to know now in our modern day.

***

Jesus often went out into the wilderness to commune with his Father in prayer. Consider the connotations of the word *wilderness*. What does this word suggest? We spend endless amounts of life's energy trying to get out of our individual wildernesses. We rarely look at what our wildernesses represent. God uses our tough times, our fires and storms, to reach out and teach us things. Truthfully, we learn much more in tempests than we do in our prosperous seasons, do we not?

When we face hardship, it is not always because Satan is against us. Christ tells us in his Word that we will meet difficulties. Such are the building blocks of the life in him that we have been chosen for. Suffering has been foretold. Life will be hard, and the path will seem wrong at times.

Each wilderness is an opportunity to take up our cross, to deny ourselves, and to endure. Doing so will lead us to a true life, albeit not the easy one our hearts desire. Yet, God's help through life's forests and fires then becomes clear. He is forging and purifying us. If we blame or get angry at God or cut ourselves off from him, we are in trouble. We need to rely on him, not on our money or on family or other people or on our status or fame.

What if all was perfect? We don't grow in those times nearly as much as in the alternative. We need to trust God and then trust ourselves to step into, face head-on, and endure life's storms. If we fail to do so, we place ourselves into a trap—that of a missed life! We need insight and wisdom. We should ask him for it and read his Word and pray. He will enlighten and lead us! This is what the Lord says:

> "Do not fear, for I have redeemed you;
> I have called you by your name; you are mine.
> I will be with you
> when you pass through the waters,
> and when you pass through the rivers,
> they will not overwhelm you.
> You will not be scorched
> when you walk through the fire,
> and the flame will not burn you.
> For I Yahweh your God,
> the Holy One of Israel, and your Savior,
> give . . . a ransom for you, . . .
> Because you are precious in my sight
> and honored, and I love you,
> I will give people in exchange for you
> and nations instead of your life."
>
> (Isaiah 43:1–4)

Our wilderness life experiences show us that we need God's care. When we truly know him, we realize how much he protects and guides us. As our lives progress, we realize more and more how involved he has been throughout. He journeys alongside us. Always remember his past provisions. They strengthen us during days of trials and dark woods.

Our wilderness experiences also confirm to us that we will receive his blessings if we will only stay the course! No matter how hard the expedition is, it will only get better from here! With each passing day, we are one step closer to our homeward goal!

***

As a teen, I greatly enjoyed war movies. Revolutionary or Civil, the First and Second World Wars, Korea, Vietnam—it did not matter. The strategies of good versus bad and heroic individual or group efforts making or breaking the cause were completely addicting. I could not get enough. I remember often setting alarms for 2:30 a.m. so I could get up and watch *Run Silent, Run Deep*, *Anzio*, or *The Battle of the Bulge* on the old black-and-white TV. I did this so often that my mother asked a child psychologist in front of a large school gathering if there was something wrong with her son!

Maybe those movies are why in younger years I often considered what I might do in the event of an invasion of America by a foreign enemy, much as occurred with Israel as Assyria came in or with the tribe of Judah when Babylon invaded. I thought it would be optimal to make a hideout in a cave or dig a tunnel and bunker complex underground. There I could hide out in total secrecy from all that was going on above, yet also come out and do stealthy commando raids for food, weapons, or whatever else I needed. I also dreamed of being out alone in the wilderness for months or more, like the long hunters of yesteryear who would disappear for long spells from society while out hunting, trapping, and exploring.

Nevertheless, as time passed, I realized we are not meant to be isolated bastions of independence. Rather, we humans were created by our Father to be social creatures. My mind changed at this realization. When bad things happen, be they epidemics, invasions, or natural disasters, what I hope would happen in all of us would be the mindset to get out rather than to hide out, to step out toward others, openly carrying our Lord's messages and comfort when they are most needed.

But need we wait for grand disasters? Why not encourage people now! Show them your true gifts of the Holy Spirit and, in particular, your faith in him, your love for them, and your reason for hope. As per 1 Peter 3:15, Christians must always be ready to give an answer to those who ask for the reason why we hope and act as we do. A world such as ours, in its present downward spiral, sorely needs this salt and light. That is our God-ordained duty!

***

We each have a story, a pathway throughout our lifetime. It meanders through dark valleys. Yet, our trail also lets us summit awe-inspiring peaks, with their amazing heights of unbelievable beauty. God is always with us through all our twisting and turning sojourns here in this world. He guides us. He proficiently leads us. Sometimes by our choices we unfortunately go into places he does not advise, places that are not in our best interest. Nevertheless, he still does not leave us.

Imagine if we each made a deliberate choice, as our primary focus in this life, to build other people up, to hack through those dense obstacles that block our way similar to the thick brush and vines we encounter in the deep woods. We have the option to simply go around or avoid them altogether. But nothing good comes from avoiding our problems. There is a better way. We can try to machete through. We can choose to be an active leader who breaks down obstacles. Imagine if we attempted to blaze trails not only for ourselves, but especially for others. What would our world look like?

In my days afield as a hiker, explorer, huntsman, and fisherman, I had the opportunity to make trails, that is, to trek through unbroken wilderness. Something about doing that deeply stirs the soul. The very consideration of such an endeavor arouses primitive, heartfelt emotions. In several places, particularly in rural Alaska, I thought that perhaps no human had ever stood in the spot I was standing since the world began.

I have broken new trails and then had to mark them for the benefit of my return trip or for others. Some blazings were as simple as placing markers to guide myself. Others involved hacking for hours with a machete through heavy brush, ripping briars, and soldiering through the tough and spiny devil's club plant of southeastern Alaska. Another time, I used an ax to chop a trail through ice blocks as large as cars to allow my sled and dog team to safely traverse Arctic ice fields.

Blazing a trail takes work. Some trails are easier than others. But, as anyone knows, once you accomplish a difficult task—especially one in which you are the leader, the trailblazer—and you advance yourself or others into new and positive territory, the satisfaction is beyond comparison!

How would you like to bring many, many benefits to others, particularly those with whom you work, study, play, and interact? How about doing so daily? Most of us want to do this! But what is the best way to go about achieving these ends? The only reliable course runs through Jesus Christ, our friend, our benefactor, and our personal Lord and Savior.

If you already know him, you need to delve deeper, getting to know him better and better. Identify, develop, and incorporate what gifts he has made available for you into your very core being. You will then receive many, many benefits and victories for yourself and for those with whom you interact daily. These will greatly help in all relationships, situations, and events, even through the hardest times.

If you do not know him, explore what he can do for you. God, our loving Father, has given us a guidebook, a map for our lifetime. It is his Holy Bible, his Word. The holy Scriptures are not pop-psychology nor a how-to book on worldly gain or other transient earthly issues. Most of us have never consulted it in detail enough to incorporate its wisdom and its promises into our actual lives. Christians often have some knowledge of God's Word, but most live life without employing it optimally; that is, without using it appropriately, for all the many benefits it provides. If you are not a Christian, you may have glanced at God's handbook, the Bible, previously. Perhaps you have even studied it in detail. Embracing it is the most important decision you will ever make!

In my prior book, *Rise and Soar*, I reviewed the trustworthy nature of God's Bible. I discussed the amazing benefits a relationship with God and his Son, Jesus Christ, confers upon anyone willing to go through the effort to seek them and their promises. Perhaps the word *effort* is not appropriate. Yes, you will have to spend time and open that very intelligent and gifted mind that God has given you. (He gave it for the purpose of knowing and interacting with him, by the way!) It is a task that becomes easier and easier and more enjoyable as you begin to see the benefits he provides while you venture ever deeper into his realm. Proceeding as such changes your viewpoint. It alters your mindset. It positively colors your relationships. It changes how things affect you. It also positively alters how you come off to others in appearance. I have had people ask, "There is something different about you. What is it?" Or say, "You look like an interesting person to know."

These benefits and gifts from our loving Father and his Son, Jesus, which I discuss in my prior volume, are their fantastic gifts of peace, real joy, fulfillment, and ultimate rescue. His rescue is twofold: it is a rescue from the craziness of this world and God's rescue from a sentence of eternal judgment. No one wants to suffer once their life on this planet ends.

***

Christians need to pray. We must ask God into our hearts, our minds, and our souls. We must petition him for his guidance and ask him to reveal himself to us. We should recall his promises in Scripture that any who seek him earnestly will find him! We should meet with groups of other believers to learn how to lead this Christian life. What is best is a biblical church based upon scriptural foundations. Also beneficial is a small group of people who live life together and study the Bible together. Further, we should strive to spend more time in Christian media—books, magazines, and music—rather than worldly media. Making these changes truly affects your inner soul. As Scripture describes, God's presence and wisdom become manifest as light shining out through your eyes into this dark world, a light visible for all to see!

In the Bible, I recommend Peter's two letters, 1 and 2 Peter. These were written for new believers in the early church, and they are still valuable today! They talk not just about praying and getting into his Word. They also tell us how to act and function daily in our brief time here. Their eight short chapters discuss and inform us of how new (as well as established) Christians are to act. And they give instructions for how to deal with those difficult issues that arise over our lifetimes.

***

Let us examine each of these promised gifts from our Lord in more detail. These are peace, joy, fulfillment, and, ultimately, rescue.

A) Peace

> "And the peace of God, which transcends all understanding, will guard your hearts and minds in Christ Jesus." (Philippians 4:7 NIV)

***

It was an early April midnight. High in the Alaska range, a brutal, Arctic, high-pressure system was pushing out the snow clouds and bringing in temperatures of negative twenty-five degrees Fahrenheit, with wind chills much less than that. Attempting to sleep in a flimsy tent without heat was difficult at best. I got up, geared up, and headed out into the deep, snowy darkness.

My friend Gary stirred and asked, "Where are you going? You're gonna be in trouble out there!"

"Gonna sit out on that mountaintop game trail for a spell" was my reply.

He warned, "You're crazy. The wolves and grizzlies are out."

"I'll be fine. I'd be happy just to see a bear. If you hear me shoot, come running," I countered.

It had been so cold that there was still four feet of snowpack. So, we had seen few predators thus far. Only their tracks. The bears had just begun to emerge from hibernation. It being one of the coldest springs on record, some had emerged but returned to their high mountain dens. Only the biggest bears were stout enough to weather the cold, yet even these stayed close to their winter dens. Sows with cubs could not leave the vicinity of their warm beds until the cold snap broke. And no living thing was dumber than the two humans out running around hunting for large male bears.

I walked a bit, then settled down in a snowbank just off the game trail right below timberline. I covered myself with the insulating fluffy white stuff until only my upper chest and arms were exposed (for easy access to my trusty .375 H&H Magnum). What unfolded next is something I will never forget.

The snow clouds were breaking up yet still intermittently spitting large flakes. The fluffy billows illuminated as they floated in and out between the half moon and a multitude of stars. The snow sparkled like billions of Christmas lights on the pines and across the valley below. A lone wolf on the mount directly opposite howled. He was answered by a pack on my mountainside. They bantered back and forth as the northern lights then began to play. The pale-pink aurora entered the dance, its green-and-white fingers adding a special touch to the amazing drama unfolding in God's heavens and on the snowy hills below.

The cumulative effect was mesmerizing. It connoted a sensation of nearly total peace, despite my being refrigerated prey in a predator's paradise. Yet, it ended all too soon. Sitting still in a snowbank in subzero temperatures can only be tolerated for so long. After two hours, I reluctantly extricated myself from the bank and trudged back to my sleeping bag.

Nineteen years have since passed, and still the peacefulness bestowed by this time in God's amazing wilds was a sensation that cannot be forgotten. Yet, this experience exponentially pales in comparison to the reassuring peace of mind that God our Father grants us when we fully know him and his Son, Jesus our Christ. Let's look further at this gift of God's peace.

***

Why me? Why are all the tragedies, this pain, this evil, still allowed to endure? These are common questions today, queries that remain unanswerable. No answer we could understand would heal our hearts. Even if we could possess God's divine knowledge of why each event occurs, we would still have our pain.

We need faith, a strong trust that God is working all for our good. Realize that even if God does not respond with whatever timing and circumstances our human minds feel he should, we must still trust him. We need his peace and comforting presence so that we may rise above and get through our trials. It is helpful here to pray not only for deliverance or understanding, but also for the gift of his perfect peace.

Peace is elusive in today's world, and it more often means no longer fighting with one another. The peace of God is much more than this. It is a mental, physical, and spiritual calmness. It emanates from the understanding that, by trusting God and having him always with us, we can endure, rise above, and outlast any trial. With such perfect peace, no suffering can ever change our trust in him!

To obtain and maintain this peace, we need to know God as our friend and heavenly Father and as our Lord and Savior. We must avoid negative thinking during even our direst trials. Such negative thoughts keep us down. They make us bitter, depressed, and apathetic. They leave us feeling squashed and like giving up. Nevertheless, if we always do our best to think positively, even in crises, by looking for the good and seeing the blessing in whatever comes our way, we can rise above bad times. It may come as a surprise, but just as steel and diamonds are forged and strengthened through continued pressure and as gold and silver are refined by fire burning away their dross and impurities, trials are ultimately positives for us. Avoid negativity. Ask God to help you remain a positive thinker in your trials. You cannot control all things in your life all the time, but you can control your attitude and your outlook. It is also extremely helpful to help others when they go through similar difficulties. By so doing, our trials help not only ourselves but our brothers and sisters as well. As it has been said, "In Christ, we have everything. If you need help, he is strength; if you are afraid of death, he is life; if you desire paradise, his is the way; if you flee from darkness, he is light. Happy is the man who hopes in him."[1]

***

Peace in our hearts and minds is difficult to achieve, especially if we are always thirsting and striving after the latest and greatest things: that newest technology, a better vehicle, a better stock portfolio, a raise, that next promotion, and so on. None of these will ever satisfy us. None of these can fill the hole inside of us. It remains ever empty until it finds satisfaction in the Lord God. Saint Augustine wrote, "Our heart is restless until it rests in you."[2] This means that we need to relinquish our continual striving to have control over every situation. Trust God's love and guidance in his shepherding! He is always with us no matter where we are or what mess we are in. Perfect peace comes only when we give our human worries and concerns to him. Trying to be strong or to control it all paradoxically leads to more confusion and chaos. We are not the center of the universe. Rather, we are mutually dependent and interconnected, with God our Father at the center. Consider Isaiah 26:3: "You will keep in perfect peace those whose minds are steadfast, because they trust in you" (NIV).

***

What would you give to have the world by the tail or to be on top of the world? Can anyone ever be like this on our crazy planet? Our mind may think of the billionaires—surely, they must have the world in their grasp, right? Yet, think of the added worries they have besides those common to all people: illness, family issues, old age, frustration, bitterness. I suspect billionaires often have psychosocial stressors beyond those of the average person, given the added stress of managing all their surplus wealth and possessions!

Now, consider this: if you have Christ and his promise of salvation, then at the conclusion of this life, don't you truly have it all? In fact, don't you even now have the world by its tail? You control it through Christ, rather than allowing it to control you. Its fickle winds still buffet you in its wild seasons, but they can never overwhelm you or alter your final destiny!

If you are a Christian, you understand that this life now is as bad as things are ever going to get for you. The best is yet to come! But if you are not in Christ, then this life, as imperfect and hard as it is, is as good as you are ever going to get. It will go badly for you as you age in this world, with all the compounding physical ailments and afflictions of time, and at the judgment, which will be much, much worse and will also last for ever after!

Real peace only comes to our human hearts when we let Christ, the true Prince of Peace, into them and then submit to him fully. We must relinquish the fight for our wills. Our human minds want to challenge his authority. It takes a conscious decision to say yes and allow him to forgive our sins. But it grants us his amazing peace and eternal life! Consider these scriptures:

> "It was through what his Son did that God cleared a path for everything to come to him—all things in heaven and on earth—for Christ's death on the cross has made peace with God for all by his blood." (Colossians 1:20 TLB)

> "So now, since we have been made right in God's sight by faith in his promises, we can have real peace with him because of what Jesus Christ our Lord has done for us." (Romans 5:1 TLB)

> "Those who trust in the Lord are steady as Mount Zion, unmoved by any circumstance." (Psalm 125:1 TLB)

> "I will lead them and comfort them, helping them to mourn and to confess their sins. Peace, peace to them, both near and far, for I will heal them all. But those who still reject me are like the restless sea, which is never still, but always churns up mire and dirt. There is no peace, says my God, for them!" (Isaiah 57:18–21 TLB)

> "I am leaving you with a gift—peace of mind and heart! And the peace I give isn't fragile like the peace the world gives. So don't be troubled or afraid." (John 14:27 TLB)

B) Joy

> "Your hearts will rejoice, and no one will rob you of your joy." (John 16:22b)

The terms joy and happiness are defined by many people in many ways. Some see these as states of contentment or as possessing the feeling that all is well. But are joy and happiness the same thing? Are they synonyms? I feel more appropriate definitions are that joy is a state of mind or a state of being while happiness is merely a feeling.

True joy is what we acquire when we establish and maintain a valid relationship with God. Joy can be imagined as looking up to God, realizing and thanking him for his blessings. From this joy evolves a true happiness that can be imagined as looking out toward others while serving as a joyous example.

Real joy consists of several components. These are, first, peace: a firm contentment that we are always in God's hand no matter what happens. Second, there must be a sense of fulfillment. We know that we have been placed by God here on this earth at this exact place and time and are doing exactly what he made us to do. And third, we need his rescue from this world's craziness into a guaranteed salvation. Peace, fulfillment, and rescue create an umbrella of true joy, as our forgiveness of sins by Christ's blood truly helps us remain persistently joyful.

This is true joy. It is not like the world's happiness—such as one has on Christmas morning or on one's birthday. Such happiness is never satisfied, and it doesn't last for long.

Pastor and author Adrian Rogers describes joy as a thermostat and happiness as a thermometer. You control a thermostat, like how you can set your own internal degree of joy. The thermostat's setting does not vary with outside conditions or temperatures. But your happiness thermometer changes as different weather systems and storms roll through. This is an excellent way to compare joy versus happiness. You control joy. You can set it at an appropriately joyful level. And if you know Christ, it persists no matter what tempests, climate extremes, or other situations are swirling around you. We will only achieve this joy, this blessing from God, if we first seek, then find, and then continue to hunger after him. He then will, as he promises, add all blessings to us!

We must come to realize and definitively know that seeking only this world's pleasures, that is, its goods, riches, foods—its stuff—cannot and will not ever meet our spiritual needs. Only Jesus can. Therefore, we must seek him if we are ever to achieve true and lasting joy and happiness.

Now, we must seek him with the correct attitude. We should hunger for him as if we are starving, thirst for him as if parched from days in a burning desert. What prevents us from doing such? Well, if you're already full of worldly desires or excessive worries and concerns, you have a distracted, unfocused mind and spirit. Thus, you are less passionate in your hunger and thirst for Christ, just as eating too many snacks minimizes your desire for food at dinnertime. Each of us has as much of God as we want. Those with small appetites get small amounts, while those with larger appetites get larger amounts of him! Consider what

Christ says in Matthew 6:33: "But seek ye first the kingdom of God, and his righteousness; and all these things shall be added unto you" (KJV).

So, we are told we must seek him first, above all else. He promises we will be joyous and receive many blessings. Contrast this with merely seeking worldly happiness in isolation. Our doing so makes God second place. We say, "I will seek God once I achieve this or earn that or become such or get that promotion or buy this thing or get married," and so on. We become trapped in a never-ending cycle of worldly desires and cares, thereby putting aside God, the one and only thing that can make us truly joyful here in our world. What a paradox!

Focusing primarily and excessively upon any desire starts a process of further insatiable hunger, just like overly rich food does. It satisfies for a bit. But, once satisfied, we soon get hungry again. So, we return, repetitively, always needing more. Why not try to focus on Christ instead and see for yourself what occurs? Once you realize what you get in Jesus, you will not be able to stay away! Strive to desire and to seek him above all else. Determine a path by which you can begin to know him better and better. As you get to know him, he fills you and blesses you, as the Bible states he will. He also seals you for eternal happiness with him, whether you pass from this life or when he returns, whichever is first.

People we meet may ask us, "Why are you so happy?" or, "What's your secret?" Christ, through the Spirit, gives us true joy that no one can ever steal away, not even in severely dire trials. Our joy will still shine out of the darkness and reveal our great Jesus to others. No, we do not have to be happy for our sufferings or our sadness. Christ was not. But we should rejoice and stay joyous overall as we recall how he stays with and supports us in and through each of these sorrows. We know how the story so gloriously concludes, and this realization makes all the difference!

Therefore, do not ever give God's joy up, even if family, financial, work, or other issues seem unalterably bad. Or, if this joy has already left you, you must realize it is gone and work toward its restoration. Ask Christ to help in this endeavor. And ask yourself, do your trials really compare in any way at all to the joy of truly knowing Christ? Consider the much more severe hardships of so many other less fortunate souls in our world. Even more so, recall the trials of Jesus himself on that rugged cross that he bore for us! And always remember 1 Corinthians 2:9: "No mere man has ever seen, heard, or even imagined what wonderful things God has ready for those who love the Lord" (TLB).

You may ask, "Why doesn't God reveal these things to us now? Then, all can know how amazing it will be." But consider the result if we knew exactly what joys awaited us in heaven. Imagine God giving the entire world a five-minute peek at his paradise. My young daughter in discussing this felt that all people would then believe in him, but I disagree. There would still be many selfish and evil people who care nothing about God or about having a relationship with him. Such unbelief was there in many of the Jewish religious elite in Jesus's day. We still see it today. And Revelation foretells that we will even see it at the end of Christ's thousand-year reign, when, despite how much better the world has become in its best millennium since Eden, countless multitudes will yet rise up to fight against God's armies in the final battle.

I also believe that if God revealed heaven to us now, many in true relationship with him would to their detriment look to check out early, especially when in bad situations such as severe chronic pain or illness, grief, or depression. We, too, would probably be much more careless and reckless with our lives.

Therefore, we are left to believe and to trust his promises. "You love him even though you have never seen him; though not seeing him, you trust him; and even now you are happy with the inexpressible joy that comes from heaven itself. And your further reward for trusting him will be the salvation of your souls" (1 Peter 1:8–9 TLB).

***

To find true joy, we must realize that God has put each of us here to know him and to make him known—in essence, to glorify him! This is the meaning of life. Our true calling is to be in a personal relationship with Christ and to develop his character as best we can in ourselves. Do not miss your true calling! If you do, you will never become the beautiful butterfly that you were meant to be. You, instead, will stay the lesser caterpillar. While serving him in your true calling, glorifying him, you will realize that each moment is a new opportunity that will never return. So, remain alert to actively engage and bring each moment to its fullest potential, that of forwarding God's kingdom work.

Every single moment spent, from actively evangelizing, to family time, and even your resting, is to be done with meaning. Each is put forth with purpose. Resist simply trying to get through that course, that workday, that meeting, that year. Do not merely endure events and the passing of time. Rather, strive to look at each moment's possibilities through God's viewpoint as his faithful follower. Emulate Christ as in Colossians 3:12–14: "Put on heartfelt compassion, kindness, humility, gentleness, and patience, accepting one another and forgiving one another if anyone has a complaint against another. Just as the Lord has forgiven you, so you must also forgive. Above all, put on love."

God at this exact point in your life is asking you to strive to do your work for his glory. He has placed you in that job, on that team, with that family, and in that social circle for definitive reasons. Realizing this improves your attitude instantly! It motivates you to your very best efforts in doing these tasks, thereby achieving optimal results. Your interactions with others are extremely important: let them always see Christ in you.

***

In summary, true joy should be a constant in every Christian's life. Happiness will come and go. While happiness is a great feeling, it only occurs when things are well with us in this world. And for most of us, this is not too often. True Christian joy never leaves you, unless you choose to lose such by sinning and turning your back on God. It stays with you always, even in times of troubles and sadness!

To achieve true joy, one must first repent and return to God and accept Christ's payment for one's sins. This gives us a joyful peace. We firmly know that there is no sin whatsoever left between us and our Lord. (Romans 5:1–2) God accepts Jesus's blood offering on our behalf, which washes away all our guilt. We then achieve real peace and joy, knowing he will do exactly as he says. Therefore, we definitively know exactly how it all ends, and we are certain that it will be great!

***

So, how is your life going? Do you have this persistent joy? If not, you need to reach out and choose it. Prayerfully ask God for it. Then, remain in daily conversation and community with him, and read your Bible regularly. You will gain this happy life for yourself. God can do all things. Choose him as your authoritative and unchanging rock. Heed the Word from our Creator. Place his wisdom far above all other noise of this world. Make the choice to follow Christ as friend and Savior. Make God's Word your guidebook for living a truly joyful life!

No matter what situation we are in, no one can ever take our joy from us. Do not let it fade! But, if you have already lost it, ask the Lord to restore it. Remember what Jesus said just before his death: "You will rejoice; and no one can rob you of that joy" (John 16:22b TLB). Strive to persistently keep this in mind, no matter how desperate, dark, or dire our earthly circumstances may become. "This is the day the Lord has made. We will rejoice and be glad in it" (Psalm 118:24 TLB).

C) Fulfillment

> "My success—at which so many stand amazed—is because you are my mighty protector. All day long I'll praise and honor you, O God, for all that you have done for me." (Psalm 71:7–8 TLB)

What is fulfillment? It is a contentment, an inner peace that we receive when we know, without doubt, that what we are doing here and now is exactly what Christ wants us to do with our lives for his kingdom. How would you like to feel fulfilled at this point in your life? How would you like to know that every single moment is being done with purpose?

Like the magi, we are searchers. We seek the true God as our life's goal, whether we admit it or not. If we are sincere and earnest, steadfast and undistracted in our search, he will guide us to himself! We must, however, avoid being easily distracted, worldly thinkers who obsess over trivial issues and fear losses (like King Herod did), such as the loss of power, family, a job, money, or relationships. When we do so, our fear declares that our security hinges on these unimportant issues that we feel we can control. Yet, in truth, we are helpless sinners who control nothing! The saddest part is that, like Herod, we may completely miss Christ. He is what is most important.

Thus, we need to change our thinking, our decisions, and our actions. We must ascend above worldly things. Then we will meet and know our one true Lord God. And he alone can give us life's answers. He is our primary treasure while we are here in this world as well as in eternity. If we are steadfast and sincere in our search for him, Christ always guides us to himself!

By faith, we continue the work of Christ that he began two thousand years ago. He commands us to act as his priests in this modern world, carrying on the acts of the Apostles and all those who succeeded them right up into our current era. As we do that, Christ and his kingdom (along with the salvation he brings) become known to more of the lost world. They are revealed through our evangelizing and our good works!

In John 15:1–27, Jesus tells us that he is the vine and we are his branches. He means that we are destined to produce good fruit if we stay with him. We must abide in Christ, he tells us—in his love and in his Word. If we do so, he promises we will bear much fruit that will glorify his Father.

Christ uses us to reach out and touch others, bringing his love and his peace, joy, and fulfillment. He distributes his hope and rescue. And then, ultimately, he delivers his salvation. He indeed is with us still!

He states that if we keep his precepts, we will abide in his love. He gives us these to follow so we will be protected and our joy will be full. He also tells us that we are his friends if we do what he commands. Yes, he is our friend, our trailblazer. He has made known to us the real knowledge of God our loving Father. Christ states that he chose us for the journey. He did not simply allow us to choose him. He has appointed us to go out and to bear fruit. Such is fruit of a permanent type, which is summed up with his three words: love one another.

***

From our limited viewpoint, it is often hard to see and understand that Christ has huge plans for every one of us for as long as he keeps providing successive breaths and heartbeats. If we are still here in this world, no matter how small, insignificant, helpless, or sickly we may feel, there is a mission he wants us to accomplish. Once our mission is fully completed, God will take us up to be with him forever.

Do you ever think, *Does my life really matter*? or, *What is my purpose*? Jesus tells his followers on mission to be salt and light.

> "You are the world's seasoning, to make it tolerable. If you lose your flavor, what will happen to the world? And you yourselves will be thrown out and trampled underfoot as worthless. You are the world's light—a city on a hill, glowing in the night for all to see. Don't hide your light! Let it shine for all; let your good deeds glow for all to see, so that they will praise your heavenly Father." (Matthew 5:13–16 TLB)

Let us look at each of these commands.

Regarding salt, the metaphoric comparison is that, just as table salt seasons food, we are also asked to season, or to change for the better, all whom we meet. Nevertheless, Jesus asks us to sprinkle our saltiness, not overload it. We must learn this distinction. Just as too much salt ruins any meal, it can destroy any relationship or discussion.

What about light? This command means we are to be representations of Jesus's light to all we meet. Light makes things more attractive but also exposes dirt or imperfection and eliminates nasty things such as vermin, bugs, and mold. Have you ever turned over a log or rock in a dark forest and watched the snakes, spiders, centipedes, and other critters scramble away? This is exactly what God's Word does when applied to all evils.

Like Christ, the true Son, sunlight improves things. It makes the world more attractive. It enhances and beautifies. Imagine a predawn mountain landscape. As the sun rises, the horizon changes from a dim, hazy outline to a bright, clear vision of pink and yellow alpenglow beauty across its snowy peaks.

In a similar way, we are instructed to instigate change. We are not meant to merely exist or coexist in some quiet and private Christian life. We simply cannot keep his light to ourselves—its news is too good! Others need to hear it, no matter how hard they fight against you, as described in Jeremiah 15:20, which states that some "will fight against you like a besieging army against a high city wall." God also assures us that these "will not conquer you, for I am with you to protect and deliver you" (TLB).

Therefore, Christians are called to be Christ's agents and to act as salt and light. Salt kept confined in its shaker never seasons anything. Light kept dimmed or turned off altogether illuminates no one. Our world needs Christians to stand up, speak up, and step out, now!

Wherever God has placed us, we are there because of him. We are in the very spot from which we are best able to fulfill ourselves and accomplish what he desires. We are to forego and forget trying to be popular in this world and instead become a changer, a moved mover. We glorify God by these actions. Because of us, someone new to Christ will want to know and honor him and, thereafter, be saved by him! He places us in our current positions for a reason. There we are asked to be his arms, his hands, his feet, and his voice—his agents of change!

In so doing, we model Christ's love, forgiveness, saving grace, and power to all we meet so that they will also want to meet him. Jesus will change them too and propel them into their true purpose and fulfillment, further glorifying our God!

Does this sound boring? It may if you have not lived it. But it is not! Adopting his plan, his outlook, and his pathway for your life puts you directly into the leading action role of an exciting, non-routine, day-by-day adventure as you stand up, speak out, and step up for him! Recall Proverbs 14:14: "The backslider gets bored with himself; the godly man's life is exciting" (TLB).

Ask God to fill you with his Holy Spirit. Yield yourself, your desires, your dreams, and your goals to his purposes. Ask him, "Lord, what do you want me to do?" Do not quench or extinguish his Spirit. Instead, ask to be filled with him and believe that it will be so. But remember, he will never enter nor fill nonbelieving, dirty hearts. So, always confess and repent, bringing your sins before God and asking his forgiveness, which he is always gracious to give! Next, simply believe and seek the Lord in his Word and in prayer, remaining always hopeful and positive in your thinking. Then watch out! Hold on tightly! Your own specifically designed, individualized adventure is about to begin. Consider these promises from your heavenly Father:

> "In everything you do, put God first, and he will direct you and crown your efforts with success." (Proverbs 3:6 TLB)

"'They are like trees along a riverbank bearing luscious fruit each season without fail. Their leaves shall never wither, and all they do shall prosper. For the Lord watches over all the plans and paths of godly men, but the paths of the godless lead to doom." (Psalm 1:3, 6 TLB)

"'For I know the plans I have for you'—this is the Lord's declaration—'plans for your welfare, not for disaster, to give you a future and a hope. You will call to Me and come and pray to Me, and I will listen to you. You will seek Me and find Me when you search for Me with all your heart.'" (Jeremiah 29:11–13)

D) Rescue

Entering the surf off Mustang Island in south Texas, I saw few swimmers. It was a beautiful day, and I was soon way out in the calm water well past everyone else. The temperature was perfect. What a day to be floating in the Gulf! I swam out a bit too far and realized I needed to head back in. As I turned back toward shore, I saw the sight most swimmers dread: people madly scrambling from the water, pulling kids along, while those ashore pointed and yelled, "Shark!"

At first, I saw nothing. Then a dorsal fin appeared, directly heading my way. No one else was in the water. The fin closed the distance and disappeared. I submerged and spun, watching my perimeter through the murky green water. I could not tell where he would come from but needed to be ready to kick, punch, and gouge at its face, eyes, and nose.

I waited and waited. Nothing. I surfaced, gulped air, and went down again. Nothing. Then, on reemerging, I saw the fin's profile not fifteen yards distant. It was heading straight for me. I went under again, fists ready. Imagine my relief when a large but well-meaning and playful dolphin's face came into view!

While some may not consider that a rescue, I do! I have had many other close calls (which I believe to be divine rescues) with polar and brown bears, mountain and African lions, wolves, and coyote packs, as well as with the natural elements themselves. Many are recounted in my first book, *Rise and Soar*.

I have also had two very close calls with firearms in the hands of others. Once on a west Texas handgun range, I was leaving my berm (set up to accommodate one shooter per lane, with dirt walls piled high on three sides). Seeing that I was packing up, a man and woman approached. They began emptying gun cases and gear while telling me that the lady had a new gun. Needing no further reason to hightail it, I told them I would be gone in a second. Nevertheless, she pulled her revolver out and promptly dropped it. The gun discharged, putting a .357 round into the large wooden table we were standing beside. It missed my leg by less than six inches. As they apologized profusely, she reached for the gun, saying, "Sorry, it's new!" My response was, "Don't touch it until I am gone. Give me five seconds!" And that was all the time I needed.

Another time, I was taking a novice hunter turkey hunting. Before leaving home, I asked and was told that his shotgun was not loaded. Reaching the field as dawn neared, we got out of my truck. He handed his gun out the door to me, barrel first. Luckily, I pushed the barrel away from my face just before he inadvertently pulled the trigger in the handoff.

BOOOOOMM!! The shell's percussion waves knocked me back a step. My ears were simultaneously ringing yet deafened. I had powder burns on my face and brows. Yet, I was miraculously unscathed!

God's rescues aside, I cannot stress enough how these are extremely important lessons that I teach all hunters and shooters, from children on upward. Every single gun must always be considered loaded until you *yourself* check to be certain it is empty. Even if another swears that it is so, *always* confirm for yourself. And never point any firearm at anything you do not wish to shoot!

***

Were these events divine rescues? Not all may agree, yet I am convinced they were. What if, while hiking a mountain trail, you found someone clinging to a scraggly branch. You saw them barely hanging on, well off the edge of a cliff, risking a precipitous drop onto sheer rock far below? Would you simply walk by and say, "Have a nice day," or would you lend a hand? Or imagine someone drowning in a lake from which you can rescue them. Which of us would let them drown? Very few would ever do so. Now, what about the people around us who do not have a friendship with (and therefore do not have the ultimate rescue of salvation promised by) God and his Son, Jesus? Aren't they also in a precarious situation on the precipice of a deadly cliff or about to drown?

We can extrapolate any life-and-death situation to being representative of a person without Jesus, one without a true relationship with God their heavenly Father. Unfortunately, if they continue throughout their entire lifetime until death without such relationship, they will be judged and sent to a place of eternal misery. Why, then, do we not approach these people with whom we daily live, play, study, and work with the same attitude we would display if they were in a dangerous physical situation from which we could rescue them? Why are we reluctant to bring them the good news of God and thereby let his Spirit and his promises change and eternally save them?

There is in truth only one completely adept and reliable guide for our lives in this world. If we fail to enlist with him, we are not safe in our travels. Think of being led by an inexperienced guide, and let's consider one specific area of expertise: bear behavior. While not a certified expert, I have spent so much time in bear country around each type of North American bear that I know what a bruin is thinking based upon its actions and reactions. And beyond my field experience, I have also read volumes of scientific research about bears' social systems, family dynamics, and behaviors. I have seen so-called experts disobey these rules, sometimes with disastrous consequences. And I have had inefficient, worn out, misguided, and lazy wilderness guides. The result is a less-than-optimal adventure that is more danger-prone along the way as well.

Some of these guides simply did not know bear behavior. Others admitted they were out of shape, often sitting in their boats all winter rather than getting ready for spring season. Others felt it was too early or too cold to go out or too far to walk to that next ridge.

Once, on Kodiak Island, I spent most of the first nine days of an eleven-day trip essentially walking the northern bays and mountains by myself. When the guide finally came out and found me, he berated me for going out alone for hours on end. He also openly admitted that he was lazy and simply wanted to lay around. But now, on day nine, he worried he could lose his license and guiding privileges were something adverse to occur if he were away from me.

I have had some poor guides who did not want to go out in the mornings while telling me, "Bears are not out then." Others told me to shoot bears that they said were legal males but clearly were female or that were much farther in range than they claimed. Another greatly desired to go to Mexico with his new girlfriend, so he wanted me to shoot a bear as soon as possible. Had I not been more aware than they, many of these episodes could have resulted in very poor consequences for myself or a bruin!

I recall a radio call to our boat in the Alaskan ABC Islands while we were hunting brown bear. The Alaska State Troopers called and asked us to check out a certain region of the Tongass National Forest. This is a rainforest that is dark even at high noon in most spots due to its heavy tree cover. They told us a deer hunter had wounded a brown bear, thinking it was a deer. They asked us to go in to see whether there were orphaned cubs. If there were, we could notify them or even bring the cubs out ourselves if they were small enough.

Tracking any wounded bruin is extremely dangerous. But I had always wanted a bear cub, even if just for several hours. So, I expected a grand adventure. The adrenaline was pumping as we moved off the beach and into the dark rainforest. The undergrowth in places was so thick you would not be able to tell if a bear was a mere ten yards away. I have had them stand up on me at such distances before, surprising both myself and the bruin! We were not making noise, instead being as quiet as possible. My guide was extremely fearful. He would take a single step, rarely two in a row, and freeze for as much as several minutes at a time. In fairness, certainly, a wounded bear is not to be minimized. They are extremely intelligent and clever. I have seen animal intelligence studies in which bears rank only below the chimpanzee and the elephant, even rating above the gorilla. And from many friends and guides, I have heard tales of wounded bears—browns in particular—circling back along their own blood trail and lying in wait for those tracking them. They often lie in thick brush or on a slight elevation above the trackers and then break out with explosive force immediately on top of their pursuers. But at the snail's rate we were going, we would never cover the required search area before nightfall. His master guide title, achieved after having done this for nearly twenty years, seemed questionable to me. By the end, we did not find any cubs or evidence of a wounded bruin.

Another time, while driving down a wilderness road late one evening as near-darkness approached, I saw multiple vehicles stopped along the shoulder. This was grizzly country. And sure enough, eight to ten people, including small children, were out of their vehicles and walking toward something in the woods. Jumping out, I could see it was a grizz and that they were all in grave danger. They were way too close at about twenty yards. Besides the squealing children, there were women in bare feet, foreigners, and other unwise persons walking into the woods very close to that bear. They were attempting to take pictures as it foraged for food.

I told them to get back, but they replied, "Oh, it is just a little black bear. It will not hurt us, will it?"

"No," I said, "that's a grizzly bear with a typically bad temper. If you get too close, he's going to come and knock you down."

"Ooh," one screeched, "will he eat us?"

"No," I replied, "but he might claw or chew on you."

Given their high-pitched voices, I explained that the children were in significant danger. I inserted myself between the people and the bear as I quickly educated them on grizzly behavior and temperament. Suddenly, they began to run, scream, and shout. I told them to keep their voices down and back away rather than run. But, as I turned back, I saw the grizz coming in on a diagonal path, directly toward me. I had gotten way too close while trying to keep these people from becoming grizzly-bite material. The bear lumbered nearby, head moving side to side, but fortunately not at all agitated or distressed. The only adrenaline spike I had was when he abruptly stopped. He peered directly at me with those beady red eyes. He was clearly wondering what I was doing there, right next to him. This was at about twelve yards. Those two seconds seemed much longer. He fortunately then swung his head and lumbered past me without exhibiting aggression or agitation at all.

This was certainly a blessing, and I use my intervention here as an example of how a wilderness guide with appropriate knowledge should attempt to help others who are not knowledgeable about things like local animal behaviors, the environment they are in, or approaching weather systems.

I, too, guide many people through forests and swamps. Sometimes, I guide children and other times, adults. These are usually people who have less experience in these realms than I. My daughter and I for several years have led groups of school children on survival hikes in which we do compass and orienteering work, hike to high elevations through thick brush and briars, make primitive shelters, start fires without matches, cook stick breads and bannocks, and teach other wilderness skills that very few people possess nowadays. Finally, well after dark, the job of the novices is to get us safely back home through those black woods using compass bearings taken earlier that day.

Throughout all such adventures, a good guide consistently places the safety of those under his care as his paramount objective while undertaking and completing any journey. For example, I also know of African tour guides and professional hunters who have taken cape buffalo, lion, or hippo charges themselves. They suffered devastating consequences and even death. But they did so from their knowledge and protective instincts, saving their clients and tourists at their own expense.

***

Now, in bear country, appropriate knowledge of bear behavior is mandatory for safe and successful passage. The bear species are notably different in their traits and characteristics. I have spent months in the field with brown and grizzly bears as well as with blackies. I have also spent weeks in the field with polar bears. Possessing sufficient knowledge of each type's behaviors, especially in territories where more than one type coexist, is mandatory to keeping safe.

Initially, if you see a bear before it sees you, you should move quietly out of sight, giving the bear a wide berth. Try to leave its immediate area, yet be cognizant and alert, and especially check behind you often to be sure it is not following. If you have a weapon or deterrent like bear spray, have it ready. And please know how to use it! Ten dollars invested in practice will pay great dividends if you ever need to use it. You need to know how to point and spray the cannister. Many unfortunates spray themselves in the heat of the moment! And being aware of wind currents—even mild swirlings—is essential, as my daughter and I found out one day in Wyoming's Grand Tetons! Also remember that bear spray can work to opposite effect; it can enrage a bear rather than deter it. Interestingly, research has shown that the best bear deterrent, even more effective than pepper spray, is to open and spin a multicolored umbrella. Most bears have never seen anything like it. And they will pause and stop charging. This is most likely a self-preservation instinct, as bears typically will not (excepting the example of a mom with cubs) take on a foe if they perceive possible risk of harm to themselves. I have carried a compact umbrella on my pack in Canada and the western states but have yet to employ it.

If a bear sees and approaches you, stay calm. Do not scream or yell. Talking quietly, for instance, "Hey, bear. Hey, bear," lets it know you are human, which may help. Back up slowly. Never run, as running triggers its pursuit instinct. And it may help to circle into the wind, especially with browns and grizzlies. This has helped me deter Alaskan brown bears who were trailing me through the wilderness.

Now, if a polar bear approaches, you must escape immediately, or you will certainly be fighting for your life. That animal, God's ultimate predator, needs every calorie it can gulp to survive its supercooled environment. With a nose that can smell you at over twenty miles distant, if it sees you, it will try to eat you. In *Rise and Soar*, I discuss in detail two nearly fatal experiences I had with polar bears.

However, deadly predatorial encounters are the exception rather than the rule with brown and grizzly bears. For those who do not know, brown and grizzly bears are the same species. A bruin is called a brownie if it lives within seventy-five miles of the coast. It tends to be a larger animal because it has access to high-calorie seafood, namely fish. Grizzly bears live inland, seventy-five miles or more from the coastline, and tend to be smaller as they need larger territories to procure the less plentiful foods in these regions (fresh game, plants, berries, and carrion).

Unlike the polar, a brown or grizzly bear, while it may be hungry enough or sick enough to eat a human if it cannot easily catch other wild game, in most cases simply wants you out of its way and out of its territory. Of course, crossing any mama bear with cubs too closely will elicit the same reaction from the mother, regardless of bear species. Yes, most brown or grizzly bears will bite, claw, and scratch their victims in a close encounter, but they rarely consume them. This bear simply wants you out of its area or out of commission, if need be.

These bears may make false charges before attacking. Yet, these warnings look very scary. The bear runs at you, huffing and puffing, head and ears up, often taking short leaps toward you and making as much noise as possible with snarls and tooth popping. Again, back up slowly. Do not run. Do not scream. Speak firmly and calmly to the bear. Try not to display fear. If possible, circle into the wind. This can allow a curious bear to catch your human scent and realize exactly what you are. I have done this to defuse several instances in which bears were following and seemingly stalking me. Once they caught my scent, they bounded away into the brush never to be seen again. And I like to think this was simply because of my human scent itself, not because I had been in the bush without a shower for days or weeks on end! Keep your eyes on the bear and stand tall with arms up. And try to avoid direct eye contact as much as possible, as this is often perceived as a threat. Looking larger makes the bear question whether it is wise to challenge you. Never lay down or kneel. Remember that the false charge is a scary bluff, not the charge to be most concerned about.

A real charge occurs when the bear puts his head down and ears back and comes straight at you quietly. That bear is going to make contact with you (unless bear spray, the umbrella tactic, or gunfire into the turf in front of the bruin deters the assault). The best thing you can do at such time is to take the hit, glancingly if possible, and then play dead. Lie absolutely and completely still. If you have a backpack on, even better. Curl up to protect your neck and head. You are going to get bitten. You are going to get scratched. Many bears even perform what I call a butt swipe at the attack's end, raking claws across the buttocks to make certain you are no longer a threat. Do your very best not to move. Very commonly, bears will linger nearby after their assault. And if they see movement, hear noise, or perceive anything else that signals that you still could be a potential threat, they can reattack, sometimes in multiple sequences.

Of course, if the bear begins attempting to eat you, that is a different story. Put all your strength into your defense. This can sometimes be the case with old bears with poor teeth or orthopedic issues, which can no longer catch their natural game, or sometimes with a young adolescent. Nevertheless, this is the exception rather than the rule with brown and grizzly bears.

While usually smaller, a black bear can be very dangerous. If he attacks, his plan is to make a meal of you. Thus, the best rule of thumb with polar bears and blackies is escape if possible. But if you cannot avoid an attack, then fight for your life. If one of these bears is biting or clawing you, he plans to eat you. Conversely, with the brown-grizzly species, the best strategy is to, again, play dead, protecting critical areas while staying very still. This species commonly stops its attack once you are no longer seen as a threat.

This is an example of the knowledge of bear behavior that any good and proficiently appropriate wilderness guide needs to keep himself and his company safe. If the trail guide does not possess or act with the correct knowledge, then the travel group is in real danger and likely to have an uncomfortable time, at the very least.

Clearly then, having an experienced and knowledgeable wilderness guide makes things easier and safer. It takes less energy and effort to get to the objective, and there is less risk of injury or danger along the path. Leading well means not only having knowledge. It also means putting the safety of others ahead of your own as you guide.

***

Let us now shift our discussion from human to superhuman guides and trailblazers. Once we recognize who God and his Son, Jesus Christ, are and what they can do for us, they become rescuers. They are our guiding beacon lights. Throughout our lifetimes, they lead us to the safe and appropriate places where we long to be. They make our trials easier to endure. They are beside us through our storms and our trails of misery. Not only does our life become a safer and calmer journey, but we can help others find their correct paths. Just as Christ is our optimal trailblazer, we become extensions of him, his assistant guides. We then bear good fruit as we lead others to the master guide himself.

Though Jesus is alongside us, he is honest about the trials and persecutions that will arise on our journey when we follow him and bear good fruit. The world hates Jesus the Christ, our guide, so we too, will have difficult times whenever we work to forward his kingdom. As our guide, he warns us not to go off alone without him. We must stay with him! One way to better weather the wind, darkness, and precipitation that rages against us is to see how Christ lived through his own trials. He was in constant conversation with God. We need to follow his example. He will safely lead us through dark woods and trouble into joy and open skies. New life will come if we match his gait. But if we leave him and get lost, we will stop bearing good fruit and even die. We must stay with him and stay in his Word. He knows the territory better than anyone. Following anyone else in our quest for fulfillment, joy, peace, or rescue will only end in disappointment and failure.

When we choose Christ as our trailblazer, we become part of his permanent and positive winning efforts. We become assistant guides and co-builders in his kingdom work. He is urging us to step into this journey. He has chosen us for it specifically. Abide, rest, and remain in Christ through the ups and downs of your pathway. If you will do so, he will remain in you, and your work for him will be achieved.

***

The trio of gifts that God grants us, namely those of peace, joy, and fulfillment, all lead to our rescue from this world. They are all we require until, ultimately, his grace delivers us for all eternity into a final rescue, that of eternal life, where we achieve a never-ending, amazing, and close communion with him!

I can sincerely say that my life with Christ has been a refreshingly happy and exciting adventure compared to how I used to try to get my happiness. If you have never tried Christ's way, his path through your wilderness, you need to. Enlist, engage, and try the experience for yourself. And recall God's promise here: "In my distress I prayed to the Lord, and he answered and rescued me! He is for me! How can I be afraid? What can mere man do to me?" (Psalm 118:5–6 TLB)

Christ will perform this saving rescue mission for us in this life. He helps us through our fires and keeps us from the flames. He will assist through our trials. And he will also protect and spare us from specific trials, although not all. Always remember that Christ rescues his followers from all that might truly endanger them: "The steps of good men are directed by the Lord. He delights in each step they take. If they fall, it isn't fatal, for the Lord holds them with his hand" (Psalm 37:23–24 TLB).

To be rescued, you must step out and seek God and his kingdom. Do not sit back and wait. Consider God's message to Judah's King Jehoshaphat on the eve of the major battle in which the Hebrews were greatly outnumbered by soldiers from Moab, Mount Seir, and Ammon:

> "The Lord says, 'Don't be afraid! Don't be paralyzed by this mighty army! For the battle is not yours, but God's! Tomorrow, go down and attack them! . . . But you will not need to fight! Take your places; stand quietly and see the incredible rescue operation God will perform for you, O people of Judah and Jerusalem! Don't be afraid or discouraged! Go out there tomorrow, for the Lord is with you!'" (2 Chronicles 20:15–17 TLB)

God in his Word repeatedly promises to strengthen and assist us in our kingdom endeavors:

> "You will be filled with his mighty, glorious strength so that you can keep going no matter what happens—always full of the joy of the Lord, and always thankful to the Father who has made us fit to share all the wonderful things that belong to those who live in the Kingdom of light. For he has rescued us out of the darkness and gloom of Satan's kingdom and brought us into the Kingdom of his dear Son, who bought our freedom with his blood and forgave us all our sins." (Colossians 1:11–14 TLB)

God also declares, "I want you to trust me in your times of trouble, so I can rescue you and you can give me glory" (Psalm 50:15b TLB).

Ultimately, the choice is yours. Are you going pursue and worship mankind's worldly creations and wisdom, that of the tree of the knowledge of good and evil in Eden, which condemned Adam and all of humanity? Or, will you choose Jesus's cross, the tree of salvation? I tell you most sincerely that only his tree, the cross of Christ, can provide real purpose in this life as well as his hope and his peace, his true joy and fulfillment, and ultimately his rescue.

Let's conclude by looking at two more of God's rescue promises:

> "Yet I will rejoice in the Lord; I will be happy in the God of my salvation. The Lord God is my strength; he will give me the speed of a deer and bring me safely over the mountains." (Habakkuk 3:18–19 TLB)

> "The Lord is good. When trouble comes, he is the place to go!" (Nahum 1:7a TLB)

***

Next, we shall look at biblical characters who provide excellent and inspirational examples of being kingdom trailblazers. None of these were perfect people. But they stepped up and stepped into the roles God had planned for them. In so doing, they produced great fruit—great results as they acted for him.

I. The Evildoer:
Manasseh (2 Kings 21:1–18; 2 Chronicles 33:1–20)

Do you know anyone who does evil? I certainly do. I stare at one such person in the mirror each morning. Unfortunately, we all fit into this category. Yet, some do evil much more than others. It may be to a much greater magnitude, frequency, or volume.

Sin can be defined as the performance of actions that are against God and his goodness. It can also be neglecting to perform actions God wants us to do. God has a plan for goodness in each of our lives. When we choose to go against it by deliberately sinning, we push the pause button on our growth remote control. Sin inevitably leads to adverse consequences and repercussions. By sinning, we reverse some of God's kingdom work in our lives. We interfere with his progress. We hinder the sanctifying, transformative work he is performing in us. The Spirit convicts our conscience to warn us, should we leave the pathway God is guiding us upon. We need to listen to the Spirit! We should not do anything against him. Rather, we should prayerfully consider exactly what

God would have us do in every situation. He is our master trailblazer. We must trust him and follow his directions and course.

We should feel frustration, disappointment with ourselves, and discouragement whenever we willingly stray off our good course into sin's snares. The Holy Spirit convicts us and makes us realize that we are losing something important by straying off the given path into the unknown darkness. Yes, the diversion may briefly seem exciting, but the consequences, we know deep down, are not worth that brief moment of satisfaction or excitement! But our hearts are human. They will make worldly choices. And this pattern unfortunately recurs many times over our lifetimes.

Yet, we only have a short time in this world. Why, then, should we waste our time groveling in the darkness? The murky bottoms are not where true joy, real peace, fulfillment, or rescue reside!

When we choose the path of darkness, we are walking toward death! We must ask God our Father and his Holy Spirit to show us the true way leading to life.

When we willingly choose the course of evil, we choose against life and goodness: we choose against God. If this does not ring sad resonances within us, we are not Christians. We should never feel good after sinning. We are volitionally straying. We are running away from our heavenly Father. Sin's aftermath should stir up a strong desire for repentance so that, thereafter, we do our very best to avoid that sin pattern. We should have such a deep regret that we never want to experience it again. And when we run back to God, we are overjoyed, like lost hikers who are finally found. This is what he wants.

***

Let's examine the story of Manasseh, whom we first meet in 2 Kings and run into later in 2 Chronicles. He was the evilest king in the history of Judah. He ran a close second to Israel's King Ahab, who is called the most wicked ruler in the history of the Jewish people.

Just what did Manasseh do? Assuming his throne at age twelve, he likely was granted too much power at too early an age. He rebuilt the shrines for idol worship that his good father, Hezekiah, destroyed, including altars to Asherah and Baal. He worshiped the sun, stars, and moon. He built altars to many false gods within God's very temple and its courtyards. He practiced witchcraft and sorcery. He even sacrificed children in the fire statue of the demon god Molech. He "shed so much innocent blood that he filled Jerusalem with it from one end to another" (2 Kings 21:16).

Manasseh's biggest sin was causing the people to stray from the Lord their true God such that "they did more evil than the nations the LORD had destroyed before the Israelites" (2 Kings 21:9 NIV). Those were pagan tribes who were in the land before Israel conquered them.

Nevertheless, like all others who seemingly have a "good run" of debauchery that seems endless and beyond judgment, this evil king finally met his sentence. God let Judah's Assyrian enemies overrun them. Manasseh was captured with hooks and shackles and taken to Babylon. In distress there, Manasseh "came to his senses and cried out humbly to God for help." We are told that "Manasseh finally realized that the Lord was really God!" (2 Chronicles 33:12–13 TLB). He prayed, and God had mercy upon him and ultimately brought him back to Jerusalem as a king once more.

Manasseh's story takes on an amazingly excellent ending. He made fortifications to the city walls. He strengthened Judah's cities. He removed all altars and images of false gods. Most importantly, he led the people in resuming true worship of Yahweh.

***

Do you know or have you ever known a person who seems evil to their core? But can we ever really know this? Certainly, we are not to judge any person evil based on their heart or motivation. We cannot stand in another's shoes. We cannot know the full magnitude of what they have been through. Nevertheless, we can judge someone's actions; we can, and we must. And in fact, we do this every day as we go about our lives.

So, while I would not judge any specific person evil, as only God can judge a person's heart, I have seen extremely evil actions perpetrated by men against their fellow man. My most graphic memories come from my prison ministry. I have known and heard the stories of men who have murdered people. Others have raped, robbed, or assaulted fellow human beings. Many of these men later felt they could never be forgiven. They felt that what they had done was so terrible that God could never excuse them of their sin. But they were—and are—mistaken.

Men and women like that need look no further than Manasseh. Despite being the evilest king of his era, he gained God's forgiveness and blessings by returning to his Lord in repentance. Amazing, isn't it! It sounds incredulous. In fact, once, as I completed a prison session on this story, several inmates astoundingly asked, "Hey, is that story really in the Bible? I have never heard that before! Wow!"

No matter what one has done or not done, our Lord is always willing to be merciful and forgiving. Like Manasseh, we must humble ourselves, repent, and return to God. He will turn his face and his shower of blessings back upon us! God, through the sacrifice of his Son, our Savior, Jesus the Christ, has already forgiven us of all sins! All he requires is that we believe in him and the sacrifice he made to cover all our sins with his redeeming blood. The only unforgivable sin, per Scripture, is to blaspheme the Holy Spirit. That is, to deny the Spirit's witness over one's entire lifetime that one is indeed a sinner and in need of the salvation God offers through Jesus.

So, what evils have you done over your days? Have you repented and given these to your heavenly Father to allow their complete forgiveness through his Son? If so, then you are forgiven. Your debt has been paid in full. However, if you have not thrown your sin load at the feet of your lovingly merciful Father, you will be in a dire place when you either die or when Christ returns to judge the world. So do not delay! Seek God and his forgiveness, which he freely gives! Pray something such as this:

> "Dear God, my Father, and Jesus Christ, I realize that I am a sinner unable to save myself. I am so happy that you sent your Son to bear the blame of my sins. Please forgive me of all past sins and help me to sin no more. I lay down all burdens, shame, and any regret that I carry from my past so that I can now live fully in and for you. I believe that Jesus is your Son and that he died for my wrongdoings. I ask Jesus to be my Lord and Savior, my guide, my trailblazer, my friend. Thank you, my dear Father, for giving me the opportunity to avoid eternal punishment. I pray this in Jesus's name. Amen."

II. The Exceptionally Wise:
Solomon (1 Kings 1–11; 1 Chronicles 28–29; 2 Chronicles 1–9)

How often do we hear someone say, "I'm too smart to fall for that religious Christianity stuff," or, "I am not able to simply believe in something unless I can use my senses to touch, perceive, understand, or in some other way physically experience it."

Do you really trust your finite little human mind, with its own small microcosm of knowledge gleaned from schooling, one or two occupations, and a few decades of lifetime experience? Would you say your mind is always fully appropriate, wise, and utterly reliable? Does it allow you to be able to completely rule out something such as God your Father and his Christianity?

***

Let us consider Solomon, whom Scripture calls the wisest man who has ever lived. God said, "I will give you a wise and discerning heart, so that there will never have been anyone like you, nor will there ever be" (1 Kings 3:12 NIV). "God gave Solomon wisdom and very great insight, and a breadth of understanding as measureless as the sand on the seashore. Solomon's wisdom was greater than the wisdom of all the people of the East . . . He was wiser than anyone" (1 Kings 4:29–31 NIV).

Solomon asked God for the gift of wisdom. And God gave him not only that but much more: earthly riches, great honor, long life, and many, many other fine possessions and blessings. Twice, he even perceived the divine presence with his own eyes! Solomon had whatever desires he wanted. He accomplished amazing things. He ruled very wisely. His architectural feats included building God's temple. He wrote three thousand proverbs and over one thousand songs. His great repute spread far and wide.

Unfortunately, none of these things helped him to end well. In contrast to Manasseh above, Solomon's story was the opposite. He started well but finished poorly. He took up the false gods of his pagan wives, who lured him away from the true God. Therefore, Yahweh told him he would take his kingdom from him after his death.

***

I do not know about you, but God has never appeared to me. If the wisest man ever in the history of our human world, with all his intelligence and blessings (he even saw the divine), was able to mess up, this does not make me feel whatsoever confident in my cognitive abilities!

I fail to see how any human mind can presume to know so much as to absolutely deny the existence of an eternal kingdom or the existence of a loving and merciful God and to dismiss the sacrifice his Son, Jesus Christ, made for us.

One must investigate these concepts objectively, even if they seem irrational at first. We can do so by spending time reading God's Holy

Bible, his living and breathing message to us. It will speak to us and reveal its truth if we spend time in it and ask God to open our eyes and ears to the message that we need to hear. This is too important to delay, defer, or deny until you evaluate it with an open mind. Check it out for yourself and ask God to reveal what he would have you know!

***

There is another lesson to be learned from the life of Solomon. We learn about it in the book of Ecclesiastes, which he authored. Solomon clearly had it all, the utmost that a person of his day and age could possess: wealth, women, and exquisite leisure. And he took on mentally challenging tasks as well such as irrigation, breeding horses, and magnificent architectural feats.

Later in his life, after trying every potential thing he could in an attempt to satisfy and fulfill him, he concluded that "there is nothing new under the sun" (Ecclesiastes 1:9 NIV). By this he means that everything is in vain or useless. He declares that all human endeavor is futile and unsatisfying, a "chasing the wind" (Ecclesiastes 1:14 NIV).

Like Solomon, we chase that same wind. We will never get to that end goal we somehow think will make everything better. Solomon had more worldly power, wisdom, and possessions than any person can attain. Yet, he was never fulfilled. This is a critical lesson. No matter what we yearn and strive for, simply getting to that point, that job, that position of respect, that level of wealth, or whatever, will never fill the empty spot inside of us.

Instead, we need to be thankful. We must view what we have as a gift from God our Father. We should not trade our few days for the worthless pursuit of worthless things, which, even if we could achieve or possess them, will never fulfill us. Only God can do so!

So, stop pursuing crazy, worldly things. They will never satisfy; their allure is stronger than their fulfillment! Once we have them, we only look for more, more, and ever more. The cycle never ends. The only thing that will satisfy us completely is a relationship with our own God and Father.

Without our Lord, without faith in his promises, everything in this world is worthless and fading away by the hour. It slips easily through our grasp and, upon death, is handed over to others. Only true faith and its fruit will remain!

Solomon possessed all that was possible for a king of his era. He jumped right in and experienced every available pleasure and activity. Yet, near the end of his life, he realized that this had all been meaningless, as futile as chasing after the breeze. Similarly, all that we do is a temporary shadow. We will all die. And then all our goals, works, and endeavors will be ancient history. Everything of this world we achieved will be soon forgotten!

Thus, in the latter years of his amazing lifetime, Solomon realized that without faith in God, everything is useless. Remember what Jesus said: "And how does a man benefit if he gains the whole world and loses his soul in the process?" (Mark 8:36 TLB).

We, therefore, must examine all we do and the motives behind why we do them. We incessantly strive and struggle to achieve some degree of comfort, security, and happiness in this world. Yet, there is no help but God!

Solomon was correct. If we have no hope or help beyond the grave, then all really is meaningless. Therefore, God is our only hope, and he promises not only his help here in this life, but also his divine rescue into eternal paradise with him.

Therefore, we put our hope in God our Father. We need to ask him for wisdom to enact an attitude adjustment relative to our daily activities! Take the time to examine how your hours, days, and weeks are divided and into what categories. Which are most helpful? Which are least beneficial? Attempt to limit activities and possessions. You will reduce your stress and clear your mind of useless clutter. And your wisdom will increase exponentially!

III. The Sexually Deviant:

Rahab (Joshua 1, 2, 6) and Samson (Judges 13–16)

In our world, sexually explicit and deviant entities constantly bombard our senses. It is impossible to completely extricate oneself from these influences for long. They are ingrained in most media and daily stimulate evil thoughts and desires deep within us. Such things definitively keep us separated from God our Father. These can severely limit our relationship with him. And they reduce the receipt of his intended blessings for us.

Let us consider the stories of two people from millennia past who lived sexually immoral lives, and then glean knowledge from their tales.

***

The book of Joshua tells us little about Rahab. It says she was a prostitute and a pagan who did not yet know the true God. She lived in the city of Jericho with a large family. Nevertheless, she took pity on and hid two Israelite spies in her house, protecting them from the local forces.

She then helped them escape over the city wall. In return, they promised to spare Rahab and her family in the pending assault upon her city.

The Israelite attack soon came. Jericho's walls came down. Every other living thing, from people to livestock, were slain. Yet, despite this violent and diffuse bloodshed and the collapse of the city wall into which her house was set, Rahab and her extended family were miraculously spared. No one else survived from her entire city. It, therefore, seems a logical supposition that only the section of the wall with her house in it did not fall in the attack.

Rahab had been faithful to the messengers of the one true Lord. In return, he protected her, as promised. Clearly, she got to know the Lord God better thereafter. When she first recounted the events of the Exodus and early conquests of the Amorite tribes across the Jordan in Joshua 2:11, her tone was fearful: "The LORD your God is God in heaven above and on the earth below" (NIV). But later, Joshua 6:25 states "[Rahab and her family] still live among the Israelites." The overall impression is that she progressed beyond a mere fearfulness of Yahweh. She developed a more appropriate relationship with him. It can also be assumed that she very likely changed her sexually deviant ways as well; they would not have been tolerated in Israel.

Rahab's story is an example of how any sin pattern, including sexual sins, can be overcome and forgiven with the help of the Lord God. As per Matthew 1:5, she is listed in the lineage of Jesus by marrying Salmon and giving birth to Boaz. Boaz fathered Obed, who later fathered Jesse, who ultimately fathered King David! Therefore, not only can sexual sins be overcome, but amazing things for God's kingdom can be accomplished by repentant sinners!

***

Samson, our second example of sexual deviance, is, per his description in Judges, not only a very strong man but also a flamboyantly passionate and prideful womanizer, with long flowing locks complementing his likely good looks.

When Samson was born, Israel had been living under the Philistine heel for forty years—ever since they sinned gravely before God. Samson appears to have been miraculously born. The angel of the Lord announced Samson's pending birth to his parents who, until then, were unable to conceive. It was prophesied that he was to be dedicated to the Lord and that the child would "save Israel from the power of the Philistines" (Judges 13:5b).

Yahweh performed great works for twenty years through Samson, as described in chapters 14 and 15 of Judges. Samson protected Israel from the oppressors in its lands. He killed thousands of Philistines, including one thousand with a donkey jawbone. The Spirit of the Lord was truly with him. It often took control of Samson and allowed him to perform superhuman tasks. Nevertheless, chinks in Samson's moral armor were evident from a young age.

In chapter 14, he is so obsessed and so severely lured by lust for worldly feminine beauty that he spurns reason. He brusquely and rudely commands his parents to "get" a specific Philistine girl as his wife. Against his parents' protest, he states, "Get her for me, because I want her" (v. 3). This initiates what appears to have been a dramatic, non-ideal relationship that culminates in the death of this first wife and her father and leads to Samson's vengeful killing of many men.

Later, Samson, judge of Israel, makes another poor judgement in his next relationship with Delilah. The implication is that it was also based on purely sexual attraction. And she is anything but loyal; Delilah betrays him to the Philistines. They pay her in silver to obtain the secret to his strength and invincibility, and Samson appears to be stupidly closed-minded to her attempted deceptions. She makes three unsuccessful attempts upon his life for her Philistine people. But even after these three failed attempts, Samson remains blindly prideful. He feels bulletproof, like he could never be defeated. Thus, he, on Delilah's fourth pleading, tells her the truth: that his hair has never been cut and that this is the cause of his strength. A fourth and final time, she summons her tribal assassins. One of them cuts Samson's hair. And Samson is finally captured.

The archenemy Philistines blind him, put him to forced labor, and humiliate him, for "the LORD had left him" (Judges 16:20). Nevertheless, his hair grows. One day as he is being made to entertain three thousand Philistines in their temple, Samson prays a final, desperate prayer. God grants his request to have his strength back one final time. He then collapses the temple, killing more Philistines than he had over his entire lifetime.

***

Samson's is a sad story. In his life, he continually put the Lord God to the test. He persisted in his sins of pride, hypersexuality, and disdain for the opinions of the wise, namely his parents.

Samson serves as a warning not only to honor the wisdom and advice of learned people, such as parents and Christian mentors, but also to never persist in sin patterns that might eventually cause the Lord our God and his Holy Spirit to leave us.

***

Compare the lives of Rahab and Samson. God used both to accomplish his kingdom works. Yet, what a contrast the kingdom achievements of Rahab make relative to the early demise of Samson! Her sanctifying faith, great wisdom, and subsequent positive life change make her story immensely different than his. Which character would you want to be?

IV. The Self-Righteous, Religious Hypocrite:

Saul (Paul the Apostle)

To the outside observer and to himself, Saul has the ideal Jewish life. Born into a wealthy family, he receives the best education from renowned religious scholars. He becomes a well-respected Pharisee. Believing he is doing right, he persecutes, imprisons, and ultimately causes the deaths of many Christians in the early days of the church.

Saul is present at the stoning of Stephen, the first Christian martyr, and was in complete agreement with his death. This led to severe persecution of the church in Jerusalem. Saul is a ringleader, "ravaging the church. He would enter house after house, drag off men and women, and put them in prison." He is constantly "breathing threats and murder against the disciples of the Lord" (Acts 8:3; 9:1).

One day, while on the way to Damascus with warrants to seek out and arrest Christians there, Saul has a dramatic and life-altering experience. He sees a brilliant light and falls to the ground. A voice says, "Saul, Saul, why are you persecuting me?" When Saul asks who is speaking, the response is, "I am Jesus, the one you are persecuting" (Acts 9:4–5 TLB). Then, Saul is made blind.

Saul endures his blindness and fasts from food and drink for three days. Then Ananias, acting on the Lord's instruction, fearfully yet obediently lays hands upon Saul, and his sight is restored. Through Ananias, God announces his plans for Saul: "This man is my chosen instrument to proclaim my name to the Gentiles and their kings and to the people of Israel. I will show him how much he must suffer for my name" (Acts 9:15–16 NIV).

Saul is immediately baptized and begins proclaiming Jesus to be the son of God and Messiah in the synagogues. This clearly amazes all who hear him, given his abrupt change of position. Saul was a Christian persecutor. Now he is an outspoken gospel proclaimer. We are told he does very well in debating with the Jews of Damascus who "couldn't withstand his proofs that Jesus was indeed the Christ" (Acts 9:22 TLB). Saul so upsets them that they plot to kill him. But he escapes and goes to Jerusalem.

In Jerusalem, as would be expected, Christ's disciples and the church are all afraid of Saul. They do not believe he has truly become a Jesus follower. Barnabas, however, stands up for Saul. He explains the story of Saul's conversion, how he met Jesus and began testifying for Christ in Damascus. Saul pursues his bold gospel conversations there in Jerusalem, so much so that the Hellenistic Jews also attempt to kill him. The disciples fear for his safety and send him to Tarsus.

At this time, Saul comes to be called Paul. The last sixteen chapters of Acts describe in detail Paul's subsequent ministry to the Gentiles. He travels over most of the known world, boldly preaching the gospel. He confronts Jews, Gentile pagans, rulers, and sorcerers. He also, through his letters and personal visits, advises, corrects, and encourages the brothers and sisters of the fledgling Christian church.

During his travels, Paul has many, many episodes in which God's providence is evident. (2 Corinthians 11:23–32) He continues to boldly proclaim the good news of Jesus Christ. This angers many, often inciting riots by Jews and pagans alike. He, nevertheless, always presents the gospel in a bold yet clear manner. He endures thirty-nine-lash floggings five times from the Jews and is beaten with rods three times by the Romans. He is stoned once and endures three shipwrecks with near drownings and countless days of exposure to the elements, including a day and night afloat at sea. He also receives a poisonous snakebite and undergoes hunger, isolation, scorn, and many other persecutions. He is imprisoned multiple times. And he finally pays the ultimate cost with his execution in Rome (traditionally understood to have been by beheading).

In the end, this self-righteous, overly zealous, misguided human being completely changed his life, his philosophy, his personality, his attitude, and his goals. He declared how he ran straight to the prize with no other intent but to win. He did not let himself get distracted by things around him. In 1 Corinthians 9:24–27, he states,

> "Run in such a way to win the prize. Now everyone who competes exercises self-control in everything. However, they do it to receive a crown that will fade away, but we a crown that will never fade away. Therefore I do not run like one who runs aimlessly or box like one beating the air. Instead, I discipline my body and bring it under strict control, so that after preaching to others, I myself will not be disqualified."

Paul's primary intent was to win the race. He minimized anything that would be a distraction to his efforts. He then surged forward, becoming God's critical instrument in reaching the Gentiles with Christ's saving news. He also wrote much of the New Testament, God's own inspired words. Through Paul as God's human conduit, God's words still inspire millions today and will continue to do so until the end of the age.

***

What would it take for us to become a Paul? What would it take to become a finely tuned, dedicated instrument to God the Father, Jesus the Son, and the Holy Spirit, primarily focused upon propagating the kingdom and glorifying God? How much of our daily routine (with the multiple thoughts, activities, and concerns that barrage and clutter our minds) gets in the way of what this life is meant to be about?

> "But one thing I do: Forgetting what is behind and reaching forward to what is ahead, I pursue as my goal the prize promised by God's heavenly call in Christ Jesus. Therefore, all who are mature should think this way." (Philippians 3:13–15)

Some may say that our world today is more complex than Paul's was. Our families need us. Our jobs are stressful and crazy. Yes, we all have families, and we all have jobs, as did Paul. We are not told much about his family after his conversion. Yet, we are told that he was a hard worker for the Lord. He also made tents. He wished to earn his wages, not simply be handed them because of who he was. He urged his fellow Christians to work hard and bring glory to the name of Christ. He asked them to be loyal and motivated employees.

In summary, we need to be constantly mindful of those things that distract, detract, and dissuade us from the life our Lord wishes us to live, a life that brings glory to him and also benefits ourselves and those around us. Paul is a model of one who was originally zealous yet completely erroneous and misguided in his thinking. He was self-righteous but not truly righteous. He thought he was serving God, when he was doing exactly the opposite: tearing down and working against the kingdom on earth that Jesus had established. Let us hope we never find ourselves doing the same thing!

I can look to my own example. I was raised Catholic, and while I am not generalizing by all Catholics as a whole, I was a religious hypocrite. Certainly, God used those years to form me into who I am today. And I greatly appreciate all the efforts and sacrifices that my parents, other family members, and those in religious orders provided to me. Yet, I was told by many members of that clergy, priests as well as nuns, that I must complete the prescribed rituals of the Roman Catholic Church (namely baptism, first communion, penance, and confirmation) to be saved. I was also told that one had to do many good things, enough good to outweigh the bad, so that, hopefully, when I arrived at heaven's gate, I would have more good grades than bad and be allowed in. My perception was that the entrance decision was to be made at heaven's doorstep, at its very threshold. What a difference this is from my understanding now. Now I know what God wants us all to know: that his Son Jesus, our Messiah, has paid the price. *Tetelestai!* All is finished! All we must do is believe in him and his saving grace! He has already beaten death and the grave and removed our eternal judgment if we will simply remain with him and in him!

We are indeed all sinners. We all need help, an assist from outside of ourselves. Until we reach this realization, we are indeed truly lost. Not too many years back, before I spent enough time in God's Word to realize this truth, I did not know how truly lost and sinful I was. I remember thinking, *Well, yes, I may have a little problem with pride and perhaps some anger as well, but I am not so bad as most people. I'm actually doing pretty darn well in avoiding all of those big sins I read about in the Bible!*

This is a very dangerous viewpoint. It makes us feel smugly overconfident when we believe that we are excellent and good people in God's view—maybe even almost perfect. Every human being believes they are good. Everyone believes they are quite rational and moderate in their beliefs, even if the exact opposite is true.

This view, however, changes as we spend adequate time in God's Word, in his holy Scriptures. There he reveals how lost and sinful we really are. This is a necessary step: we must recognize our extreme sinfulness and our need for a savior. That is, we must realize the fact that without him, we can never achieve heaven!

Simply being good will not get any of us into heaven. Remember the common colloquialism: heaven is not for good people; it is for forgiven people. Not one single human can ever achieve heaven by himself. We all must have Christ, who takes God's punishment for us and, in return, gives us his blameless garments of righteousness. If we refuse to accept his gift in this life, when we die, we are granted our life's choice of judgment. We become forever separated from God and are cast into eternal hellfire!

Consider other religious hypocrites. Self-righteous men and women who are not friends or followers of God and Christ exist in all ages. In the time of Jesus and Paul, these were many of the Pharisees, Sadducees, scribes, and other religious leaders of the Jews. They did not honor God with their hearts. They presented false worship with merely their lips and their blatant displays of "holiness." They desired the praise of others for their open sacrifices and penances. They did not have, as is still the case with many in our era, eyes or ears that could see the true kingdom.

Yet, God's kingdom is among us now. We need to gain the ability to see and perceive that his kingdom is indeed here in this world. While it will be much better in the future, the kingdom is with us in the present. Christians are the evidence and the extension of his kingdom. Therefore, we must be certain that we are performing appropriate and genuine kingdom work.

We should strive to see, through Paul's story, the journey of faith and sanctification that we should all be on if we are truly servants of the one Lord God and his Son, Jesus the Christ!

V. God's Friend, Yet a Sinner:
David (1 and 2 Samuel)

The church was growing by leaps and bounds. The Bible was preached. The congregation overflowed the moderate worship hall. Amazing things were being accomplished for the kingdom of God through Jesus Christ. Donations were pouring in. The funds were used for local and international missions as well as other kingdom works. It seemed nothing could derail the progress in what was the most popular church in town. Its popularity was not because of any secular worldview, such as we see in some popular churches presently. These embrace non-biblical things for fashion, and, unfortunately, such worldly attractiveness can warm the human heart. The heart is then allowed to rationalize that God might allow such aberrant behaviors.

Nevertheless, it came out that the pastor was having an affair with a deacon's wife. As would be expected, everything went completely off the rails. I heard repercussions of this from patients and friends, including some who were being counseled for similar sexual sins by that very minister. People were enraged. Others, embarrassed. Many felt betrayed or, even worse, abandoned. At that time at least, many wanted nothing else to do with Christianity, with the church of Jesus Christ, and with Jesus himself.

What a grave sin! Yet, this process continues to recur today in Christian churches. The problem is that while we attempt our best to emulate Christ, none of us is Jesus himself. Therefore, problems such as lust, greed, theft, adultery, and the like still occur enough to be brought to the forefront of our minds. Even if sin only occurs in one or two of the churches we attend over our lifetime, it leaves a bitter stain and a sour taste. The hopes and prayers are that the mature Christian will be able to rise above and realize that the offender, whether of the congregation or in a position of church authority, is not Jesus. We must not allow sin to cast doubt or do harm to our own faith.

I recall vividly another flourishing church in which the pastor urged the congregation to save one week's household salary for a project the church was trying to accomplish. We were given one year's advance notice. And the event was greatly publicized over the entire year prior. Yet, with just two weeks remaining, a sudden admission came out one Sunday about a high-ranking church member who had misappropriated a very large sum of church funds for personal use. He had stolen the money for something he wanted to do and reportedly planned to pay it back before anyone found out. While he was repentant and promised to pay it back, this undoubtedly had a negative effect upon many families who had scrimped and saved their dollars over that past year toward the gift they planned to give. While the final contribution was still amazingly large, it is difficult to know how grand it might have been had this unfortunate event not occurred.

***

Most often remembered as a man with a true heart for God, David lived a life replete with many blessings. He lived a great adventure and was dearly loved by God his Father. God's protection and providence are evident time and again throughout his many trials and difficulties. Yet, he was also a sinner. David sinned to an extreme degree at times, including the sins of adultery and murder.

We first meet David in 1 Samuel 16 when he is anointed as Israel's future king. We see from the very beginning how blessed he is. He is greatly admired by King Saul and can soothe Saul's affliction from the evil spirit that torments him. And we know from his youth the great victory over the Philistine giant, Goliath. David accomplishes this amazing feat by defending God's honor from the giant's blasphemies. He trusts that God will deliver a mere boy from the champion warrior of an entire nation.

Saul's son Jonathan admired and loved David. 1 Samuel 20:17 says, "Jonathan once again swore to David his love for him, because he loved him as he loved himself." Jonathan gives up his rights as heir to the throne to protect and warn David about Saul's plans to kill him. Jonathan pleads for David before his possessed and unstable father. He even disobeys Saul's direct order to kill David. How telling of David's charisma and blessed life that Saul's own son chose David's side over that of his natural father!

David's life becomes a wild and crazy cat-and-mouse chase with Saul. Yet, God reveals his great providence. Time after time, he rescues David, whereas the mentally unstable Saul blunders his way into more sin and is killed with three of his sons (including Jonathan) on Mount Gilboa by the Philistine army.

David then becomes king of Judah. His first task is to quell the house of Saul's claim to the throne. In a civil war, David emerges victorious. He becomes king of Israel and unifies the two kingdoms. He reigns a total of forty years, the last thirty-three over a united Israelite nation.

God makes a pact with David. He tells him, through the prophet Nathan, "Your house and kingdom will endure before Me forever, and your throne will be established forever" (2 Samuel 7:16).

David then begins a sweeping tide of great military victories against the archrival Philistines. He also subdues the Moabites, the king of Zobah, the Arameans, Amalekites, Edomites, and Ammonites. He is essentially undefeated, being unbeatable with God at his side: "the Lord made him victorious wherever he went" (2 Samuel 8:14b TLB).

But David begins to make mistakes. While at his palace, on vacation from battlefront duties, he sees Bathsheba, the wife of Uriah, bathing. Overcome with lust for her, he sets forth a plan that results in the sin of adultery. Then, to keep her husband from finding out that she is pregnant, David gives an order to place Uriah at the front of the battle, knowing that he will be killed (and he was). David adds the sin of murder to adultery.

David then tries to continue functioning as if all is well. He puts these major sins out of his mind as best he can—until the prophet Nathan confronts him. David realizes how gravely he has sinned against God, sin that had severe and life-changing consequences. He repents and is forgiven by God. Consequently, the son he conceives with Bathsheba is taken from him.

Then David's family begins to have situations in which he should intervene but does not. These grow into major dysfunctions. His son Absalom revolts against him. His daughter, Tamar, is raped by her brother Amnon. David himself sets up the event by assenting to Amnon's unusual request for his sister to come and "make cakes" in his presence, which is in his bedroom. Tamar moves in with Absalom following the rape. Scripture says, "When King David heard what had happened, he was very angry" (2 Samuel 13:21TLB). But David does not intercede.

David's next mistake is allowing Amnon and his other sons to attend Absalom's invitation for a gathering two years later. There, Absalom kills Amnon. King David's other sons flee, although it is first reported to him that all his sons have been killed, which causes him greater grief.

David grieves for Amnon while Absalom flees to Geshur. Three years later, Scripture says David longs to see Absalom but does nothing to ease the situation. He exacerbates the tension when he allows Joab to bring Absalom back but on the condition that "he must never come here. I refuse to see him" (2 Samuel 14:24 TLB). This circus continues for two more years. Absalom is finally granted an audience with David but only after a desperate tactic: Absalom burns Joab's barley field!

Absalom, by his own device, becomes popular with the people. He tells them his father, David, has no time to listen to their problems, and he begins to settle their disputes. He warmly greets all who come near. Scripture says, "So in this way Absalom stole the hearts of all the people of Israel" (2 Samuel 15:6 TLB).

Absalom then ignites a conspiracy to become king. He takes soldiers to Hebron and declares himself its king. And instead of addressing the rebellious upstart and maintaining his rule, David abdicates. He flees Jerusalem. Yet, "all the people followed him," and "everyone in the countryside was weeping" as his column marched by (2 Samuel 15:17, 23). David has six hundred men; he outnumbers Absalom three to one! Yet, he refers to his son as "the new king" (2 Samuel 15:19). David runs away—all too easily relinquishing his divinely ordained kingship to his revolutionary son against the wishes of his people and Yahweh's plan.

David has relationship and family issues that he never attempts to correct or address. He does not make wise decisions. He plays a passive-aggressive role. He sits back rather than stepping in. He has major responsibilities that he badly neglects, including his office as his nation's king. And he certainly flails and fails as a father. David does not make appropriate decisions or provide wise counsel or even seek an audience with the involved parties to mitigate bad consequences. David's poor judgement and apathy lead to tragic outcomes.

Nearing death after his initial refusal to confront the aspiration of another son, Adonijah, to the throne, David declares that Solomon will rule. He appears to have finally learned his lesson. In doing so, he deters what looks to be a bloody civil war for his throne. Adonijah peacefully submits to his dying father's request, avoiding further bloodshed and strife. David's kingdom then enters its golden age of peace and prosperity under the lead of his ordained son, Solomon.

***

This section of the Old Testament always saddens me. At times it drives me batty, because one can plainly see what is happening all around David, yet he fails to react. I want to step into the arena and intervene by giving him wise advice.

Yet, in David's mistakes, we also see a lesson and a warning to us. We see the folly of not adequately or appropriately addressing the issues that arise in our relationships with family, friends, and colleagues. Whether we are parents, siblings, friends, colleagues, or anything else, we have a role to play where God has placed us.

As parents, we need to step up and intervene whenever we see our children straying or needing advice. As spouses, friends, church or small-group members, teammates, or business associates, we have an obligation to those who meet us. We need to act with true wisdom, which is biblical enlightenment. There is no substitute for this type of discernment. It brings appropriate understanding and judgment into our activities, our deeds, and our speech. It allows us to provide superior counsel, reassurance, and comfort. It also instigates positive expectations and responses from others. Consider how David lost the respect of his children after his affair with Bathsheba. And surely rumors spread as servants and other palace staff saw these incidents with their own eyes. Their once-admired holy king was now conniving, stealing, and murdering to satisfy and cover up worldly lusts and shirking kingly and family responsibilities.

***

On the positive side, David stepped up to meet all military challenges. He made wise decisions and acted on them promptly when it came to battle strategies. Goliath was necessary for David to become a known figure in Israel. While the hulking warrior intimidated many, David had no fear. He was filled with that calming and supreme confidence that comes from knowing you are with God and he with you. How else could one confidently declare, "The Lord who saved me from the claws and teeth of the lion and the bear will save me from this Philistine!" (1 Samuel 17:37 TLB).

Sometimes God puts a Goliath in our path so that he can elicit the David within us! David likely had at least a bit of fear and apprehension as the conflict with Goliath drew imminent. Most of us would. Yet, he stepped up and completed what Yahweh needed done. This brought an Israelite victory and elevated David into the position needed to later become king. And it was his kingdom from which Christ's incarnate person would derive. In short: no Goliath, no glory, for either David or God (in this circumstance, at least)!

God still directs our steps, big and small. He is our providence and our protection. No car wreck, no weapon, no pneumonia or cancer, not even any nasty modern virus can take us out of this world until our job here is done and he is ready for us to come to him!

Current-day Philistines must be recognized for what they truly are: obstacles we must face and conquer so we can further God's kingdom purposes. He will always deliver us from them!

***

Another lesson is that when all is going optimally for David, he loses his way. When dependent daily upon God to rescue and to lead him, David is always successful, always protected. Yet, once he becomes king over the entire nation, a powerful man with his enemies internally and externally vanquished, he badly slips and falls. This pattern is clear in many examples from our modern era as well. Once we become successful or rich or famous or generally well established, we must not relax or let our guard down! This is when the enemy is happiest, as he sometimes can sneak an arrow through a chink in our Christian armor, strong as it may seem.

***

David's path through life clearly demonstrates how God preserved him. God did so because he had a plan for David. David would further Yahweh's kingdom, and David realized this. He kept in close daily communication with his Lord. He relied fully upon God's providence. How else could this young man have survived not only bears and lions in the field but the encounter with a heavily armed and armored giant as well? How else could he have escaped the many attempts on his life by a determined pursuant King Saul for so long? And how else did he emerge unscathed through so many battles with pagan foes?

The only valid answer is he kept his focus upon his Lord God. Yes, he messed up. He did so quite badly at times. He was human, just as we are. Yet, despite his failings, he rose again and again because he humbled himself. He repented. He returned to God. He turned his heart back to his Father. And God answered. God blessed David throughout his life.

His lesson is timeless. We, likewise, must realize our sins, repent of them, and return to God our Father. He is always there, awaiting our turn of heart and mind. No matter what we do, no matter how heinous or malevolent, we always have forgiveness waiting on us. This does not mean that we take sins, especially ongoing or serial sins, lightly. It may be tempting to say, "Just one more time," or, "Just this once and then I will say I am sorry." We must try to avoid this. As Christians, we are held to a higher standard. Unlike those who do not know Christ, we know the commands God has laid out for us. If we disobey, we do so foolishly, at our own risk. Every sin has consequences. These may take time to develop, or they may be sudden, swift, and devastating. Nevertheless, we know that fallout will occur whenever we sin. The Father knows all, and because he is a holy Lord who cannot allow sin to stand in his presence, we cannot come to him and remain in our sinful states. All sin must be punished.

Yet, our Father is not only holy. He is also extremely loving. Therefore, he provides us an escape from the clutches of sin. Sin seeks to condemn us to separation from our God, but God sent his Son to take our place and exchange his pure righteousness for our sinful guilt. God, thereby, proves that he considers us his friends when we, as David did, develop a true heart for him.

VI. The Afflicted Sufferer: Job

Over my third of a century practicing medicine, I would say that ALS, or amyotrophic lateral sclerosis (also called Lou Gehrig's disease, after the late New York Yankees slugger who made the disease common knowledge), is the closest thing I have witnessed comparative to the suffering of Job. I had a very close friend and colleague die from this and have taken care of many, many ALS patients, including family members of friends with this affliction.

While not as painful as other conditions nor as immediately devastating, it unfortunately has a progressively inexorable and merciless course. Death is inescapable, occurring typically in one to three years. Rarely, its relentless course continues much longer in milder variants with slower progression, but most people are dead within three years from diagnosis.

The ALS disease process arises from the gradual death of motor neurons, those cells in our brainstem and spinal cord that allow us to use our arms and legs, to speak and swallow, and even those cells that keep our lungs breathing. There is yet no cure. There have been two treatments released over the past twenty years. And while they may delay things slightly, they cannot save a person from this inexorably progressive ailment.

The disease begins typically with slurred speech and limb weakness as muscles start to atrophy, that is, to shrink. Coordination dwindles. Walking becomes impossible. Swallowing is affected. The ultimate demise is typically from suffocation when the lung muscles simply stop working. Death from aspiration of food or liquids is also unfortunately common. During this process, bedsores, bladder infections, and pneumonia are commonplace as the patient gradually becomes more bedbound. Unfortunately, it usually comes down to a decision about whether to go on a ventilator or not. The choice is a difficult one. A ventilator can prolong life by breathing for the person's severely weakened lungs. Yet, is that perceived to be a quality life?

I have cared for people with this condition who decided to stay on a ventilator for eleven years or more. They still had their mental faculties but, by that point, typically could not speak. They communicated with me and family members using eye movements. Nevertheless, the great majority, over 98 percent in my experience, do not choose prolonged ventilation as mechanical means to stay alive. They feel the quality of a life paralyzed and bedbound with breathing and feeding tubes, completely dependent upon others for total care, is not worth it. This is an individual decision that must be weighed and made by each person and their family in their best interests and according to their beliefs. There is no universal right or wrong.

What also makes ALS so devastating is that it draws itself out for so long. The afflicted person knows they are going to die—and relatively soon. But it is not a quick death. It is a slow and agonizing death. Thus, it is difficult to come to terms with. The ability to breathe gradually ebbs away until it can no longer be naturally sustained. And while there is typically little physical pain, imagine the emotional toll that ALS takes upon the person, their family, and friends. To see a loved one's life slowly drawn out of them, day by day, week by week, and month by month, is a torture I do not have words for. No words adequately describe this.

Another issue is that, among medical professionals, we often say, "ALS never affects bad people, only very good people." While certainly not universally true, it holds true for every single person I have seen with this disease. That is, the patient is an amazingly good person (at least, as much as any human can be good). They are not getting into the typical troubles that many others do over their lifetimes. While this generalization certainly does not hold universally, I am using it to make a point. Simply ask any medical professional about their ALS patients, and I am certain you will hear the same.

Therefore, a common question of the ALS patient and their family is typically, "I lived so well, took care of myself, and did not do bad things to my body, yet I still contracted this disease. Why is this happening to me?"

Unfortunately, it is a question the human physician cannot answer. Only the good Lord has this answer. The question is similar to those Job asked in the oldest biblical book (estimated to have been written about four hundred years prior to Moses's Pentateuch). And these are the same questions that humankind still asks today.

***

What was your worst day ever? When you lost your job or made a major mistake? When a family member or friend died unexpectedly? When someone disappointed or badly betrayed you? Maybe you suffered a major injury or received a dire medical diagnosis and prognosis?

The first chapter of the book of Job describes perhaps the worst day that any human being ever experienced. First, his oxen and donkey herds (each five hundred head strong) are stolen and his herdsman killed. His seven thousand sheep are burned up in a lightning storm, and the servants with them are killed as well. Next, we are told that his three thousand camels are stolen, and still more servants killed by the Chaldeans. Later that day is the biggest blow: the death of his seven sons and three daughters in a house-collapse tragedy.

Have any of us had a day such as this? Have you ever lost your entire wealth and all your children in one single day? In a stunning example for us, Job's response in verse twenty-one is truly amazing: "Naked I came from my mother's womb, and naked I will leave this life. The LORD gives, and the LORD takes away. Praise the name of Yahweh."

Job's response appears to have been immediate. How many of us could ever get to the mental state required to make this decree, even if given time and perhaps some counseling? Can you imagine declaring this immediately after such tragedy and loss? Job realizes God had given him all that he had. So, he rightly understands that those things were also God's to take away from him.

In chapter two verse seven, Job's next affliction is "terrible boils from the sole of his foot to the top of his head." Job sits in ashes and scrapes himself with broken pottery, being no doubt as miserable as a youngster with diffuse chicken pox. I was eight years old when I contracted it, and I remember the illness as vividly as if it were yesterday. Given today's vaccine, many younger persons will fortunately never experience this pox. The closest comparison I can make is to diffuse systemic poison ivy with the addition of high fevers. Imagine that bit of poison ivy you get on your leg or hand being all over your body with its weeping sores and diffuse itching. Then add in the fevers and severe muscle aches common to viral infections. Yet, Job in his suffering remains without anger or open questioning. In verse ten he says, "Should we accept only good from God and not adversity?" While he does ask God to end his life, Job never sins against the Lord in his words or deeds:

> "As long as my breath is still in me and the breath from God remains in my nostrils, my lips will not speak unjustly, and my tongue will not utter deceit. . . . I will maintain my integrity until I die. I will cling to my righteousness and never let it go." (Job 27:3–6)

In chapters thirty-eight through forty-one, God speaks. He firmly puts Job—and us—into our rightful place. God declares exactly how minuscule, unnecessary, and truly powerless we are. Then, in chapter forty-two, Job rescinds some of his words and repents in dust and ashes. Job realizes the truth about God. He understands who God is. Yahweh accepts his repentance and restores him. He doubles the number of Job's flocks and livestock, and he grants Job ten more children! As the book of Job ends, we are told that he lived another one hundred forty years.

***

The lesson for us is that the Lord our God is always on his throne. He is always righteous. He is always loving. And he is willing to forgive and restore us if we will only repent and return to him.

Why, however, must bad things, tragic events, and evils continue to rear their nasty heads in our lives? These entities pursue and plague us throughout our worldly existences. Such questions are not adequately answerable from the human viewpoint and perspective. Yet, we must trust that the Lord is using all things to work together for good to those who know him and walk with him (Romans 8:28).

Through all trials, Job keeps the appropriate perspective. He realizes his place relative to God in this world and confesses that the outcome is positive, good, and already accomplished. He keeps his focus on his Redeemer. We must do the same. Then, we will be able to reply as he did in Job 19:25–27:

> "But as for me, I know that my Redeemer lives, and that he will stand upon the earth at last. . . . Yes, I shall see him, not as a stranger, but as a friend! What a glorious hope!" (TLB)

VII. The Self-Perceived, Powerless Weakling:
Gideon (Judges 6–8)

Do you ever feel as if you are in the throes of a mighty river, being tossed by its whims and powerless to change your current surroundings or destination? Do you ever feel you are too weak to be used as an instrument of our amazing and powerful God? Such a perception is clearly understandable, given the current situation of our world today. We are completely inundated with media and current events from all over the globe. We see so many tragedies, natural disasters, sicknesses and plagues, crimes and evils. Their cumulative onslaught has the negative effect of overwhelming our minds and our drive to accomplish kingdom goals. With such a flood of negatives, we seem but leaves caught in a whirlpool. We feel powerless. Who are we to be able to calm the waves, let alone alter their currents or consequences?

Let us look at the story of one who felt like this. It comes from the book of Judges. Here, the nation of Midian is oppressing Israel. The Midianites, as well as several other tribes, continually raid and loot Israelite villages to the point that people start hiding on mountains and in caves. All their livestock are taken, as are any crops. They do not have enough food to eat. That's why the Midianites are described as a great swarm of locusts who enter the land to waste it. Soon, the people cry out for mercy from God.

God calls the young man Gideon to be his instrument of deliverance while Gideon is threshing wheat in hiding, trying to keep it secret from the voracious invaders. The angel of the Lord appears and states, "The LORD is with you, mighty warrior!" (Judges 6:12).

Gideon does the equivalent of looking over his shoulder and saying, "Who? Me? Who are we talking about?" Gideon's confusion mirrors Israel's perception that, although the Lord safeguarded them out of Egypt, he has since abandoned them to Midian.

But God's response is Gideon. Gideon himself is the Lord's answer to his nation. He tells him in 6:14 to "Go in the strength you have and deliver Israel from the power of Midian" and concludes, "Am I not sending you?"

Gideon protests that his family is the weakest in his tribe and that he is the youngest member of his father's house. The Lord reassures Gideon that he will be with him and that he will assist him in striking down Midian.

Still not satisfied, Gideon asks for a sign. He presents the angel of the Lord the gift of a goat and bread, and the angel of the Lord brings fire from a rock that consumes the offering.

This event clearly gives Gideon some confidence. That evening, he ventures out and destroys his father's idolatrous altar to Baal as well as an Asherah pole. He then builds an altar to the true God on the same spot and offers a burnt sacrifice upon it. Of note, still not fully confident, Gideon does this under cover of night.

The next morning, the pagan men discover that Gideon is the responsible party. They come after him. Yet, Gideon is saved by the Lord through the reasoning of his father, Joash.

Gideon then conscripts an armed force. Yet, he still displays poor confidence in himself and in the power of the God of his fathers as he asks for further proof—two more consecutive signs over two evenings. He lays out a piece of fleece (wool) on the first evening, and he says that if, in the morning, the ground stays dry but the fleece is wet with dew, he will know for certain that God will deliver Israel.

Amazingly, despite the solid affirmation of God's reassuring sign, this doubter delays one further day. He asks for the sign to be performed again in reverse, that is, for God to keep the fleece dry and the ground wet. God patiently performs both signs, just as the questioning and still unsure Gideon requests.

Then, finally confident that God is with him, Gideon takes 32,000 soldiers to confront the invaders. God then asks him to let all but 300 warriors go home so that it will be clear to all that it is God's hand granting the victory.

Performing a brilliant night assault, Gideon and his 300 men surround the Midianites, Amalekites, and Qedemites. They are severely outnumbered by 120,000 foes! Still, they blow their trumpets and break clay pitchers with torches inside them. They simultaneously shout, "A sword for Yahweh and for Gideon!" They throw the entire enemy force into utter chaos. God turns their enemies upon each other, and they flee. Israel pursues them. Four Israelite clans join in the rout. All culminates in a stunning victory. Their enemies are annihilated.

Gideon then displays great wisdom and humility. He declines the people's request to become their ruler: "I will not rule over you . . . the LORD will rule over you" (Judges 8:23).

Yet, he promptly shows his human heart as well, asking for all to donate gold from their plunder. With this, he forms an ephod (mimicking Aaron's calf in the wilderness), a sacred vestment. He then displays it in his hometown, sadly turning Israel's victory into idolatrous sin: "Then all Israel prostituted themselves with it there, and it became a snare to Gideon and his household" (Judges v. 27).

Nevertheless, Gideon's story ends positively, as we are told he does keep the peoples' faces turned toward Yahweh for the remainder of his days. Unfortunately, once Gideon dies, the people promptly return to Baal worship.

***

Even in the chaos of an occupied nation (one controlled by locusts, no less), God continued to perform mighty works. Moreover, these were clearly from God's sovereign hand, not because his instrument Gideon was such a mighty man or a brilliant military strategist.

Throughout Scripture, God repeatedly used the few to defeat the many. He used the poorly educated to outwit the worldly wise. He did these things so that we may clearly see that the victories indeed were the work of our Lord. No sane person would attack 120,000 men with a meager 300! It is, therefore, evident to all that these triumphs were not done through human power or wisdom.

How often do we feel like Gideon—completely overwhelmed by the pace of our world and by the ongoing hurricane of events? Do you feel powerless to alter your situation and relegated to simply going with the flow? Are you merely reacting to events as they occur, as opposed to trying proactively to change them, to alter such for good, to minimize negative fallout, and to reduce the evils of our planet?

We exist in a tumultuous world of multiple confusing messages and signs, a world in which it is difficult to find our one appropriate and optimal path, our best course through the gloomy forest's trees. Yet, there is a solution. In fact, there is only one answer. And your heavenly Father is calling to you with this solution right now.

Through Gideon, God clearly demonstrated how he can use anyone and anything to bring about his kingdom work. Our physical prowess, cognitive abilities, possessions and wealth, societal position, or lack thereof, do not matter. Fix your eyes as well as your mind, your heart, and your soul solely upon your only Savior. He will employ you in his mighty work of bringing about his kingdom here on earth, resulting in an exciting expedition for the remainder of your days here!

You will become God's own trailblazer through this dark world. You will assist in bringing his light to its dim corners and beneath its rotten logs. While there are no more Midianites or Amalekites such as Gideon faced down in days of yore, there are innumerable other challenges and obstacles. What better adventure could one ask for?

As we engage, we become a part of the building of his kingdom here in this world. We also help others reach it for eternity! God is asking us to use the gifts and talents he has given us to beat back every obstacle and depravity. As we do, we reduce their adverse effects upon ourselves and our fellow human beings.

Say yes to your God's recruitment call! Enlist with him today. Then, take some quiet time alone with him. Listen. Allow him to place within your heart and mind what he would have you do. He routinely uses the seemingly weak, the ineffective, the too small to accomplish amazing things! If we remain with and in him, God will use us to achieve his desired ends.

If you accept his challenge, I promise you will not be disappointed. Rather, as Gideon discovered, God can always be trusted to fulfill his promises. Our Father does not abandon his own. Become his sword today, as Gideon and his men cried, "A sword for the Lord!" You will be amazed as well as powerfully heartened at the results!

VIII. Timid Evangelists and Fearful Prophets:

Moses and Jeremiah

A. Jeremiah

In Jeremiah 1:4–8, Jeremiah's ordination begins with God's word that he had chosen Jeremiah before he was even formed in the womb to be God's prophet to the nations. Jeremiah's response is worth noting and is a statement we all make:

> "But I protested,'Oh no, Lord, GOD! Look, I don't know how to speak since I am only a youth.'
>
> Then the LORD said to me: Do not say,'I am only a youth,' for you will go to everyone I send you to and speak whatever I tell you. Do not be afraid of anyone, for I will be with you to deliver you."

The Lord tells Jeremiah that he has filled his mouth with his words and appointed him over nations and kingdoms. The Lord's next command is as follows:

> "Stand up and tell them everything that I command you. Do not be intimidated by them or I will cause you to cower before them. Today, I am the One who has made you a fortified city, an iron pillar, and bronze walls against the whole land . . . They will fight against you but never prevail over you, since I am with you to rescue you." (Jeremiah 1:17–19)

God desired his people to realize their sin, repent, and return to him. He designated Jeremiah in his day as his instrument for that specific people group. In like manner, God now asks us in our current era to be similar devices for positive kingdom change. We are asked to be representatives, even bearers, of his kingdom to our present age. God's message is always the same, no matter the prophet: realize you are sinning, repent of it, and return to your Father. Correct the relationship. Consider Jeremiah 15:19: "If you return, I will restore you; you will stand in My presence." Also, look to Jeremiah 29:11–14:

> "For I know the plans I have for you"—this is the LORD's declaration— "plans for your welfare, not for disaster, to give you a future and a hope. You will call to Me and come and pray to Me, and I will listen to you. You will seek Me and find Me when you search for Me with all your heart. I will be found by you"—this is the LORD's declaration—"and I will restore your fortunes and gather you from all the nations and places where I banished you"—this is the LORD's declaration. "I will restore you to the place I deported you from."

B. Moses (Exodus, Leviticus, Numbers, Deuteronomy)

Now we move to another reluctant prophet: Moses. His well-known story begins with affliction and slavery in Egypt. And it ends with those he shepherded for forty years through the wilderness at the very brink of finally crossing into God's promised land.

We all know the story of Moses, the Hebrew infant born during Israel's exile in Egypt. Rescued from the infanticide that Pharaoh had decreed for all Hebrew baby boys at that time, he is plucked from the Nile and adopted by Pharaoh's daughter. He grows up as Egyptian royalty, yet Moses maintains a love for his own people. This is evidenced when he kills an Egyptian who strikes a Hebrew. Moses's homicide causes him to flee Egypt to avoid execution. In the land of Midian, he marries Zipporah and begins his own family.

But Moses is not to have a peaceful shepherd's life. God appears to him through a burning bush. He informs Moses that he is to return to Egypt as God's messenger. There, he will tell Pharaoh of the Lord's plans and lead the Israelites out of their misery. He is told that their destination, their new home, will be a promised land flowing with milk and honey.

Resisting even more than Jeremiah, Moses presents multiple arguments for why he is a poor choice to go. He asks, "Who am I that I should go to Pharaoh and that I should bring the Israelites out of Egypt?" (Exodus 3:11). God assures him at that point that he will be with him.

Moses then replies that he does not know the name of God. He wants to be able to tell the Israelites a specific title. God replies that he is I Am Who I Am, that is, Yahweh, the God of Moses's ancestors. God then gives him specific instructions on what exactly to tell Pharaoh and the people.

Yet, Moses again shows reluctance. Fearful he will not be believed or obeyed, he whines that others might doubt God actually appeared to him.

Yahweh changes Moses's staff into a snake and back again. He also makes Moses's hand leprous and heals it just as quickly. God reassures that he will be with him and will reveal signs such as this to convince unbelievers.

Still reluctant and timid, Moses presents a fourth excuse for why he should not perform the task God ordained for him. He states that he has never been eloquent and is slow and hesitant in speech.

At this further uptight plea, God finally begins to have his patience wear down. He more emphatically, it seems, states, "Who made the human mouth? Who makes him mute or deaf, seeing or blind? Is it not I, Yahweh? Now go! I will help you speak and I will teach you what to say" (Exodus 4:11–12). Ever resisting God's call, Moses next retorts, "Please, Lord, send someone else."

Scripture notes that the Lord's anger here burns against Moses. Yet, God recommends bringing Aaron, Moses's well-spoken brother. Finally out of excuses, Moses takes Aaron back to Egypt to begin the plan God has predestined.

Next, the story progresses through a stubborn Pharaoh, disbelieving Israelites, and multiple plagues and afflictions upon the Egyptians. The plagues culminate in the death of the Egyptian firstborn, at which time Pharaoh releases the Israelites under the lead of Moses.

Yet, Pharaoh again changes his mind and pursues them, resulting in Israel's divine salvation through the Red Sea and the utter destruction of the Egyptian army.

Moses next deals with complaining, stubborn, idolatrous, and rebellious Hebrews in the desert. God provides whatever they need, be it water, manna and quail as food, and even salvation from the attack of the Amalekites. He provides a healing rescue from poisonous snakes. He even forgives the people and Aaron of their grave idolatrous sin: the creation and worship of the golden calf.

We see multiple times where Moses is depressed and frustrated, in particular following the golden calf event. Yet, he skillfully intercedes for the people with God. God threatens to destroy the disobedient complainers and make Moses a great nation instead. Moses, however, counters that if God does so, other nations would ask why the Lord brought his people into the desert to kill them. Through his reasoning and discussion with Yahweh, he saves Israel from utter destruction.

Moses next sets up the foundation for the Jewish nation. This includes the sacrificial system, the building of the tabernacle, the establishment of the priesthood and holy days, as well as multiple other rules and ordinances, in addition to the Ten Commandments themselves. He also takes a census of tribes.

As they near the promised land, Moses sends scouts to assess the terrain and its people. Unfortunately, ten of these twelve spies (excluding Joshua and Caleb) give negative reports. They are so strongly admonitory that they convince Israel to disobey the Lord. That is, the people fearfully decide not to enter the land of Canaan. When Moses, Aaron, Joshua, and Caleb try to convince them otherwise and thereby squelch this rebellion, Israel threatens to stone them.

As a result, God once more threatens to destroy Israel. Moses, a second time, intercedes successfully for the people. He quells God's anger once more. Nevertheless, Yahweh decrees that none of that generation, save Caleb and Joshua, will enter the promised land. God thus condemns his nation to forty years of wandering in the desert wilderness.

Unfortunately, even Moses later becomes part of those denied access to Canaan. This occurs because he disobeys God's order to speak to a rock at Meribah to draw water from it. Aggravated at the complaining people, Moses instead strikes the rock twice.

***

Despite the Meribah event later in his life, Moses became one of the greatest men of God in the entire Bible, indeed, in the history of this world. He was present, along with Elijah, at Jesus's transfiguration. He physically saw God's glory and regularly discussed issues with him directly. He even successfully interceded for his people. Through his discussions, Moses in effect gave Yahweh time for thought before destroying the Hebrews. Clearly, no man can change the mind of God. Yet, what appears to have happened is that Moses, by noting God's mercy, forgiveness, and greatness, perhaps provided time for God's anger to cool and soften.

***

We see a common pattern with Moses as we did with Jeremiah, one that occurs in ourselves as well. Reluctance, refusal, and excuses seem to be part of our human makeup. Our human hearts seek to keep us in a comfortable and safe context rather than taking the risk of stepping out into the great unknown.

Nevertheless, we must continually remind ourselves that God our heavenly Father has only the best intentions for us. These include his specific plan for our lives—the exact reason why he made us. If we do not listen to him and do not step into that appropriate role whereby we can fulfill his plan, we fail miserably. We fail not only God but ourselves as well. Yes, we may feel as if we are more comfortable and entertain less risk by taking our own preferred way. Yet, in so doing, we rob ourselves of fulfillment and the true joy of doing exactly what we have been created to do.

Listen to your Father. You can trust him. He has only the best intentions for you. Dedicate ample time to learn what plans he has for you. And then, once he points these out to you, do not complain or make excuses or delay. Step into the role he has designated for you. Remember, he promises that he will be with you always. He will tell you what to say. He will guide you in what must be done. There is no need to be fearful. He will protect you. Being God, he never can and never will go back on his promises: "I will be with you, just as I was with Moses. I will not leave you or forsake you" (Joshua 1:5).

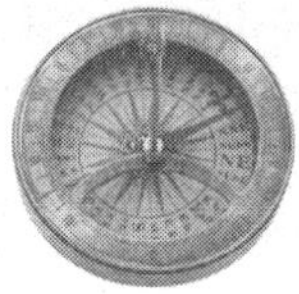

IX. The Wealth-Obsessed:
The Rich Young Ruler (Mark 10:17–31)

Mark's Gospel tells of a man who comes to Jesus and asks what he must do to gain eternal life. Jesus's initial response is to declare the Ten Commandments. To these, the man, clearly a good man in his intentions, replies that he has kept all of these over his lifetime.

Jesus understands this man's heart; we are told that Jesus loves him. He loves him so much that he points out his one apparent major fault. There remains one wall he has not yet broken down. It is a barrier that keeps him from a full relationship with God. Jesus tells him to sell all he has and give to the poor so that he will obtain heavenly treasure instead. And after that, he says to the young man, "Come, follow me." But the man's love of wealth holds him back. This young nobleman loves his wealth above all else.

We are told that the man is saddened (some translations read stunned) by Jesus's response because he owns many things. He makes the biggest mistake of his life and walks away from Jesus and his offer to follow him.

Men in other parts of the Gospels (for instance, the man from whom Jesus exorcised the multitude of demons) begged to follow Jesus. Yet, Jesus denied their requests. Here, he extends an invitation, but his offer is declined. Who knows what might have happened had this young man followed Christ. He might have had a profound role in the formation of Jesus's kingdom here on earth in its initial stages, as did the other disciples.

Instead, we never again hear of this rich young man. Did he have regrets? Did he ponder Jesus's words and give up his wealth? He more likely lived out the rest of his days in the lap of luxury with his fine foods, clothing, entertainment, and leisure.

But did he fulfill his true potential? Think of the exciting adventure the rest of his life would have become had he joined Jesus's troop and journeyed in the fellowship of Christ and the early church. He would have seen many miracles. He would have dwelt directly in the presence of and lived immediately beside God for the remainder of Jesus's life in this world. He would have experienced the joyful entry into Jerusalem and the Last Supper. He, too, would have endured the agony of seeing Jesus crucified, but then would have experienced the immense joy at the resurrection. How amazing a life that would have been! To the hind-sighted view of any modern-day Christian, how huge was his missed opportunity!

***

Would any Christian today, knowing what we now know, have refused this invitation? What would you give to see even one of Jesus's minor miracles or to speak with him for five minutes, let alone live and travel with him for several years? The one miracle I personally would choose to experience would be the glory of the resurrection. Imagine seeing and speaking to the risen Christ, he who defeated death!

Certainly, in retrospect, if he could go back, this young man may have chosen the alternate path. That is, he may have accepted Jesus's invitation. Yet, as far as we know, he never did. It is even sadder to think that he may have missed eternal paradise altogether because of the stumbling block of his worldly wealth.

Let's extrapolate to our present world. How many traps, shackles, and stumbling blocks do we have that interfere with the call of Jesus and our answer to his invitation? How often do we put his calls aside, minimize them, or perform half-hearted efforts at his commands?

Like the rich young man, we strangle our productiveness for God's kingdom. We minimize the exciting adventure we would otherwise have were we to live our lives primarily for Jesus and his kingdom's progress. We need to develop eyes that assess every life situation, to see what may be holding us back. This list may include our family, friends, work, wealth, sports, and leisure. There is an innumerable list of possibilities in every life. The main question we need to ask is, are any of these taking up so much of our time that we are limiting our efforts in responding to the call of our Lord?

This is a common fault of every human heart. None of us is different, although some have more perspective and the ability to scale back excessive activities. Indeed, if we are devoting more time to any other person or thing besides Jesus and his work, that person or thing has become an idol for us.

We need to continually assess our lives to be certain that we are minimizing our idolatry. Without limiting it, as Jesus notes, it is very difficult to enter the kingdom of heaven. Nevertheless, as he reassuringly states, "With God all things are possible" (Matthew 19:26). Christ assures us that even if we leave our home, family, or any other objects or possessions, we will receive even one hundred times more and gain eternal life for ourselves.

Nevertheless, like the rich young ruler, we have hang-ups. These are personal castles and towers, strongholds for our worldly bauble stones and hoarded jewels that are not of Christ himself. When we concentrate too intently upon them, we lose our focus upon the true rock, the only one who can fulfill and satisfy us! We perceive only what we are focused on, what we see and hear and feel. We ignore the divine and celestial, despite its greater benefits of a sound mind and a peacefully satisfied heart. We, instead, focus on our stuff, remaining mired in our little society and within our big culture.

This world's deceitful promise is that its goods, including food, money, sex, pleasure, leisure activities, and the rest are adequately fulfilling if we can just get enough. These are referred to in the Bible as lusts of the eyes and the flesh. Simply look at the advertisements in magazines and on television as prime examples. Only God can truly fill us. Thus, we must give up our stuff first, our strongholds. Then we will gain so much in return that we are fulfilled. We will never lack or have need with Christ.

We need to decide, when we see Christ before us, in ourselves and in others, exactly what we are going to do. Do we drop our stuff and embrace him? Or do we turn away, desperately clinging to our worldly objects and issues, yet remaining unfilled, desolate, sad, confused, and even abandoned?

Remember, our creator God made everything we can see, touch, feel, taste, hear, and smell: all that we experience in this world. They are his, even if we claim ownership for the brief wisps of our earthly lives. Seeing God as the center of all things (rather than ourselves) changes our view. We must ask for the Spirit's wisdom to open our eyes and ears and minds. We must take time to pray, to study Scripture, and to listen to his still small voice. Then we realize that we are all together, body and mind, in Christ. This makes it easier to disengage from our hang-ups and holdbacks so that we can achieve this relationship!

You, thus, will experience the real ruler's kingdom here and now. And you will realize that you are actually in the world, no longer of it, as you selflessly love others as much as yourself, as Jesus has commanded.

The rich young ruler saw and heard and experienced the real Jesus. He approached Jesus because he realized that, despite all his possessions, something was missing. Eternal life was within his grasp, yet he, sadly, did not reach out and claim it. Christ asked him merely to give up his idol, his money and his possessions, and follow him. He was trying to get this man to perceive that if he would give up what was holding him back, he would be truly fulfilled. We ourselves must learn the lesson of his example and do our best not to repeat this young nobleman's mistake.

X. The Depressed:

Elijah (1 Kings 17 to 2 Kings 2)

We first meet Elijah the Tishbite when he prophesies to evil King Ahab of Israel. He tells the king there will be no rain for years unless ordered by Elijah himself. God provides for him through the drought. He hides Elijah by a wadi and has ravens bring him bread and meat.

Once the water dries up, Elijah is told to go and stay with a specific widow. She has no food, save a last bit of flour and oil. Nevertheless, she shares what little her family has. She is then blessed with flour and oil containers that never go empty. She is further blessed by God through Elijah when he brings her dead son back to life.

After three years without rain, the Lord instructs Elijah to visit Ahab. The king is looking for Elijah everywhere. Ahab calls God's prophet the destroyer of Israel. Elijah says that Ahab is the real culprit and tells him to bring his four hundred and fifty prophets of Baal and four hundred prophets of Asherah to Mount Carmel. There, Elijah, the only remaining prophet of Yahweh, challenges the Israelite people. He also challenges the false prophets to build an altar upon which a bull will be sacrificed. The challenge is to call on the name of each deity and prove which is the true Lord. The call is for the true God to light the fire and burn up the sacrifice.

Elijah lets the false prophets go first. They build a wooden altar, then plead and dance all day, yet without progress. Elijah then builds a stone altar. He lays the firewood and sacrifices his bull. He also douses the entire offering with water three times. Then he calls on Yahweh, who promptly brings down fire to consume the burnt offering as well as the wood and stones. The fire even dries up the water in the trench around the altar.

The people then realize their great mistake. They praise Yahweh as the true God. Elijah orders the false prophets killed. He then tells Ahab to prepare for a coming rainstorm.

Ahab's wife, Queen Jezebel, threatens to kill Elijah after he eliminates her prophets. We are told that Elijah runs for his life in fear. He flees to the wilderness. He is clearly fearful and depressed. Sadly, he prays for God to end his life. The Lord, however, strengthens him with bread and water. This physical improvement brings about a restoration of spirit, and Elijah is told to go to Mount Horeb. There, he encounters God. He is instructed to anoint Hazael and Jehu as kings of Aram and Israel, respectively. He is also told to anoint Elisha as his prophetic successor.

Elijah later foretells the deaths of Ahab and Jezebel after they conspire to murder a man named Naboth in order to take his vineyard.

Elijah then passes the torch as God's major prophet to Elisha. Elijah is taken up into heaven by a chariot of fire in a whirlwind. He and Enoch are the only two biblical characters who are reported to pass directly to heaven without dying physical deaths.

***

In this world, do we sometimes get depressed? Really? Perhaps the better question is, how can we not get depressed when looking at all that occurs around us! So much of what swirls about us each day is adverse, negative, and often crushingly disappointing.

As a neurologist who also receives board certification in psychiatry, I see multitudes of depressed souls as patients each year. The psychiatric disease spectrum is difficult to treat. It is even harder to significantly improve. Most physical diseases will also induce depression, given their pain, limitations, and handicaps on one's activities. And while medications can help—sometimes dramatically—I tell my patients that pills alone cannot cure their depressions or anxieties. My view, after treating these persons for over thirty-three years, is that one can never overcome these afflictions adequately, nor persistently keep them at bay over the long term, without the help of God and his Son, Jesus.

Consider our prophet. Despite his dramatic victory, Elijah enters deep depression when he flees for his life from the threats of the evil queen. His sadness persists even though God speaks to him regularly and cares and provides for him many times. How often do lesser issues in our world get us depressed and anxious? This is what our human hearts tend to do. If that can happen to a prophet of the Lord who spoke to God and clearly saw Yahweh's providence time and again, how are we to deal with it in our world?

The only way to joy is by having a full relationship with our loving Father and his Son, Jesus our Christ. Such provides a real and calming peace, along with true joy and fulfillment. This relationship also provides a rescue, both from our world and eternally. Do not hesitate to seek him to ease your downtrodden spirit!

XI. He's So Unusual (The Eccentric Man of God):
Elisha (1 Kings 19 and 2 Kings 13)

How often does God use people who seem odd or unusual to the majority? I propose he does this as often as there are different personality types amongst us. Let us next examine the story of one such character from 1 and 2 Kings, a man named Elisha.

This gentleman was God's chosen successor to the great Elijah. In looking at his story, I believe all would agree that he certainly had a multitude of amazing events and experiences. His story is a classic example of the exciting adventure that I propose our lives become when we dedicate ourselves to living the life God calls us to live and to performing the duties he asks us to undertake. If we do that, we can become, as did Elisha, one of his pathfinders: God's trailblazer.

We first meet Elisha at the end of 1 Kings. Here, the great Elijah calls the young man from his plowing. Elisha promptly slaughters his oxen and cooks them with the wood from his plow yoke. He then follows Elijah and serves him as a prophet prodigy.

Elisha then gains combat experience. He witnesses Israel's victory over Aram and Ben-hadad. He is present for the Naboth vineyard incident with Ahab and Jezebel. He witnesses God's prophecy being fulfilled by their deaths. He then watches his master get taken up in a whirlwind to heaven.

Elijah asks what he could do for Elisha prior to leaving. Elisha's response is, "Please, let me inherit two shares of your spirit." Here, Elisha asks for leadership among the prophets of God, and his request is granted. Elisha then initiates his grand adventure in style. He immediately picks up Elijah's cloak and, with it, parts the waters of the Jordan River. Other prophets recognize that his master's spirit has passed to him, and they bow down and defer to him as leader.

Elisha lifts the curse God had placed on the water and fertility of the Jericho region. The city residents complain to him about Jericho's poor water and infertility issues. He asks for a bowl of salt. He throws it into the water and declares that the Lord has healed it so that it will no longer lead to death or infertility.

Next, Elisha is mocked by a gang of boys while walking to Bethel. Most commentaries say this gang was in all likelihood young men or at least teenagers. They were not young innocent children, and as a group, they were likely dangerous to passersby. They mock Elisha's hairstyle, chanting, "Go up, baldy! Go up, baldy!" Not one to be mocked, Elisha curses them. Immediately, two she-bears emerge from the woods and maul forty-two of Elisha's tormentors.

We further see God's power and Elisha's prophetic abilities when Israel's evil King Joram asks good King Jehoshaphat of Judah to help him fight a Moabite rebellion. Jehoshaphat wisely asks for Elisha's input. But Elisha scoffs at wicked Joram. He tells him to ask the false prophets of his parents, Ahab and Jezebel. Nevertheless, because good King

Jehoshaphat is in the fight as well, Elisha agrees to help. He commands them to dig multiple ditches, which God will fill with water. He also states that Moab will be handed over to them. True to prophecy, the water arrives and Israel annihilates Moab. They destroy their cities and throw stones over the good land, just as God instructed. They also stop up all the springs and cut down the good trees.

In another miracle, a widow in great debt tells Elisha her creditor is about to take her sons as slaves. Elisha tells her to procure as many empty containers as she can. He then instructs her to pour her single jar of oil into each. She keeps pouring, and the oil keeps flowing. She fills container after container until all are replete. When the poor woman reports this to Elisha, he tells her to sell the oil to pay her debt.

Elisha fulfills more prophecies and miracles in the name of the Lord throughout his lifetime. A Shunammite woman is kind to him. She gives him room and board whenever he passes by. He, in return, asks what he can do to help her. She has no son, so Elisha prophesies that she will have one by one year hence—another prediction that comes true. One day, years later, the boy, out with the harvesters, complains of a severe headache. He likely had a ruptured brain aneurysm, as he died later that day. His mother puts him on Elisha's bed and runs to the prophet. Elisha prays and, through God, brings the youth back to life.

Elisha masters food issues as well. A foolish apprentice prophet puts poisonous gourds into a stew. On eating it, the men soon realize they have eaten a toxin. They beg Elisha to help. He has them get some meal. Once added to the pot, the food is edible and no longer dangerous. Elisha also multiplies twenty barley loaves into more than enough for one hundred men.

The tale of Naaman displays Elisha's healing of a doubting pagan. The Aramean army commander, Naaman, suffers from the affliction of leprosy. But Naaman is healed and converted. He declares faith in Yahweh as the world's only God.

Another time, when some prophets are building themselves a larger home, a borrowed axe head falls into the Jordan. Elisha throws a stick in and brings the sunken tool to the surface.

My all-time favorite Elisha adventure is his tangle with the Aramean (Syrian) King Hazeal and his massive army. The king is frustrated because Elisha persistently foresees his strategic troop movements, allowing the Israelites to repeatedly thwart his battle plans. The king sends a huge force to capture the prophet.

Elisha is at his residence with his young prophets-in-training. One of these, arising early, sees the massive army and fearfully informs his master. Elisha's response is one for the ages:

> "'Don't be afraid, for those who are with us outnumber those who are with them.'
>
> Then Elisha prayed, 'LORD, please open his eyes and let him see.' So the LORD opened the servant's eyes. He looked and saw that the mountain was covered with horses and chariots of fire all around Elisha." (2 Kings 6:16–17)

As the surrounding enemy force advances, Elisha prays, "Lord, please make them blind," which God promptly does. Elisha then leads the entire army to the Samarian capital. Once there, he asks and God grants that their eyes be opened.

The Israelite king then—as I expect most of us would consider—wants to execute the Arameans. Elisha, however, forbids it. Instead, he commands a feast be prepared for the enemy.

Imagine now the disarmed prisoners of war. Their sight restored, they realize they are in the capital city of their enemy, surrounded by armed Israelites. Surely, they expect imprisonment, torture, and even death by the sword. How surprised are they to receive not just mercy but a banquet party as well! After they are released and return home, we are told that these Syrian raiders never return to Israel's territory thereafter (although, later, different Aramean raiders did afflict the land once more under another king, Ben-hadad).

Consider how those soldiers reasoned about being treated so well. In that day and age, capture for a soldier typically meant death. Why were these men so different? Surely this evoked in many Arameans a search for the doctrines, the ideals, and the God of these merciful men. I would wager that their act of kindness won many converts to Israel's Yahweh.

Later, Syrian king Ben-hadad invades and lays siege to Samaria. The starving populace within the walls begins paying exorbitant sums for bird dung and donkey heads. After exhausting these edibles, they turn to eating their own children.

Casting the blame for these dire circumstances onto the man of God, King Joram sends his best captain to behead Elisha. Elisha calls out the evil regime and promises that by morning God will provide ample food once again. The doubting captain is loudly incredulous. Elisha prophesies that the soldier himself will see it yet not partake of it.

At dusk, God produces the noise of an immense force of soldiers and chariots. This frightens the besieging Arameans. They fear Egypt and the Hittites are attacking. They flee, leaving their tents and animals, gear, food, treasures, and all else that would hinder their withdrawal. They cross the Jordan and beat a hasty retreat all the way back home. When the starving Israelites realize the food and drink of the Aramean camp is there for the taking, they stampede out of the gate and trample the scoffing captain. They loot the enemy camp and have food aplenty. So, Elisha is spot on in his prophecy once again.

Elisha later anoints Jehu, son of Jehoshaphat, king of Israel. With this, the Lord means for Jehu to kill Ahab's dreadful wife, Jezebel, and her son, King Joram. Jehu thereafter eliminates all of Ahab's evil lineage. God's decree also means that he is to kill Judah's evil King Ahaziah. So, the men of both nations rally and unite under Jehu. Even those caring for Ahab's seventy sons give them up to be slaughtered. All that was prophesied by Elijah and Elisha regarding the fall of the house of Ahab and Jezebel comes to pass.

Jehu further rids the realm of evil by killing the families and friends of Ahab, Joram, and Ahaziah. Then he kills all the prophets of Baal. He destroys their temple and converts it to a latrine.

Elisha's last recorded prophecy is to Israel's King Jehoash. On his deathbed, Elisha asks the king to shoot an arrow out the window. He declares that it is the Lord's arrow of victory over Aram. The Lord will thus deliver Syria to Jehoash. Elisha then dies and is buried.

Yet, even posthumously, Elisha continues to accomplish amazing things. His very remains retain the miraculous power of the Spirit of the Lord: while digging a grave, a Moabite raid causes the diggers to hastily put the corpse into Elisha's tomb. The moment the deceased touches Elisha's bones, he comes back to life!

***

Elisha lived an amazing and favored life, because he lived his life primarily for his Lord God. Once again, a major premise of this volume is that if we will do likewise, even though we live in a modern world, we, too, will see amazing things and experience great adventures during our lifetimes.

God uses average, everyday, common people to achieve his grandest of works. Just look at Elisha, out plowing a field! Look no further than so many of Jesus's uneducated disciples, called from their fishermen jobs. Rahab was a prostitute. And great King David was a lowly shepherd!

But you may say, "Those people all lived in the biblical cultures of bygone eras. Things are different today!" However, God has shown throughout all of history that he uses all types of people to accomplish his tasks and plans. In most cases, these were simple and common people, not nobility or top scholars. What those people had was that they were available, and they listened to the commands given to them. They then stepped out. They faithfully completed the tests required in their tasks. And they were, in the end, not disappointed.

Can any of us deny that we desire a change from the same old and dull grind—a chance to live an exciting and adventurous life free from day-to-day boredom and routine? It sounds attractive and enticing, does it not?

Therefore, why not give it a try? As Elisha did, say yes to God's call. Listen. He will tell you what he needs you to do. And, once he tells you, be certain to step out and do it!

XII. The Brash Bigmouth:
Simon Peter

Peter is portrayed throughout the New Testament as one who was clearly outspoken. He often spoke without thinking. He blurted random and poorly appropriate words (such as suggesting they construct three tents at the Transfiguration) just to say something. He commonly put his foot into his mouth. He comes off as overly self-confident, brash, and even arrogant.

Peter, too, was physically impulsive. He was aggressively protective as well. Consider how he grabbed a sword and slashed at those who came to arrest Christ in the garden.

Yet, Jesus clearly saw these qualities as appropriate building blocks. They simply needed to be tempered for the right purpose. He forged Peter into the apostle he needed to stabilize his fledgling church and bring his good news to the world. This common, uneducated fisherman was, through the Holy Spirit, transformed into a brilliant speaker and writer in the ways of Christianity.

We first meet Simon Peter in the Gospels. He is one of the first two of Jesus's chosen followers, along with his brother Andrew. At Christ's call, he immediately leaves the fisherman's life, including a massive catch of fish sure to be financially beneficial to his family. For a common laborer, that alone is a major decision.

So, Peter is with Jesus from the very beginning, experiencing his many miracles, parables, and teachings. They certainly have many discussions. Peter sees Jesus instantly resolve his mother-in-law's febrile illness and feed thousands from mere morsels. He witnesses Christ calm the night storm and expel legions of demons in the Gerasenes. He even sees the widow's son, Jairus's daughter, and Lazarus all awake from death. And how impressionable do you suppose seeing Jesus's transfiguration was!

After such, Peter is emboldened enough to ask to walk to Jesus on the stormy sea one night. However, his yet-weak mortal mind is evidenced in the fact that the storm's ferocity causes him to lose focus. He takes his mind and eyes off Christ. He then begins to sink. Yet, he wisely cries, "Lord, save me!" And that is exactly what Jesus did!

Despite this—and Peter's clearly not understanding Jesus's parables without explanation—he blatantly declares that Jesus indeed is God's Son, the Messiah! Jesus praises his answer and states that God the Father revealed this to Peter.

Yet, soon thereafter, Christ sternly rebukes a still non-understanding Peter. He even calls him Satan! As Jesus foretells his own impending death, Peter declares, "Oh no, Lord! This will never happen to You!" (Matthew 16:22). Peter still thinks that the Messiah is going to establish an earthly kingdom. He could not comprehend that the Christ must suffer and die.

Showing his humanness further, Peter then undoubtedly takes part in the disciples' discussions of which of them is the greatest. And he probably joins them in shooing away the children who flock to Jesus. He even asks what people who leave all for Jesus will receive in return! (Matthew 19:27) Jesus of course corrects the disciples' attitudes in the first two events and goes on to reassure them of the great reward awaiting them.

At the Passover meal, Jesus again explains his course and tells his disciples they will all run away and abandon him. Peter boldly declares that no matter what happens, he will never do so: "Lord, I am ready to go with you to prison and to death" (Luke 22:33 NIV). Jesus replies that Peter will deny him three times before morning! If Peter had not made that bold statement of swaggering bravado, is it possible that he may not have suffered such a blatant episode of thrice denying Jesus? No doubt, that night of denial stayed with him for the rest of his days. It was likely his life's most dire regret.

Fortunately, unlike his associate Judas Iscariot, Peter repents of his denial. He returns to Christ and, over his remaining days, achieves great benefits for God's kingdom. Just as Jesus saved him from drowning in the storm, he redeems Peter from his denial. Judas, on the other hand, overly distraught from his betrayal, never attempts repentance or begs forgiveness. Instead, he takes his own life to end his pain and misery.

Peter stays in the courtyard during Jesus's trial, and we are not told anything else about him until resurrection morning. Did he shutter himself away in the upper room with most of Christ's other followers? This seems most likely, as only John is mentioned being close at hand during Jesus's death on the cross. Could Peter have been in the background watching the walk to Golgotha and Jesus's execution from afar? While possible, it seems unlikely for a man who so adamantly declared loyalty yet broke and denied the one whom he knew was God's own son. I suspect he had a guilt wound so deep that he felt completely crushed. This feeling was then undoubtedly added to by the loss of the friend who had been his master and teacher over the amazing three prior years.

Also, consider Peter's regret about being unable to stay awake in the garden of Gethsemane following the Last Supper. Three times in the garden, Jesus woke him. Jesus clearly asked Peter to stay up and pray with him. Yet, each time, Peter fell asleep. He must have regretted missing those last few hours with Jesus. He simply slept them away! How often must he have longed for those few hours over the remainder of his lifetime?

Yet, after his errors, consider how overjoyed Peter was on resurrection day! While he was incredulous at the report of the women that Jesus was risen, he ran to and was the first to enter the empty tomb. Though he likely didn't fully understand what had occurred, imagine his immense joy at seeing his friend and Master alive again!

Yet, there certainly was great angst and guilt. Peter had betrayed his Lord, the Son of God! Would he be punished? Would Jesus forgive him? Imagine the tumult of joy mixed with great regret and even fear that churned through Peter's thoughts. He likely heard the news of Judas's demise. And betrayal and denial can arguably be mentioned in the same breath. Would Peter also pay for his error with his life? Or, worse yet, would Jesus reject and condemn him? Peter knew the stories of God's wrath against sin, and few sins could be as great as denying God's own Son. Peter had heard Jesus's very words, "If anyone publicly denies me, I will openly deny him before my Father in heaven" (Matthew 10:33 TLB). The forgiveness of sins brought about by the new covenant of Christ's sacrifice was not yet understood, even among Jesus's closest followers. Peter had every reason to fear. Yet, early one morning, Christ forgave Peter.

As a prelude to this exchange between them at the Sea of Tiberias (Galilee), Peter and five others of the original twelve disciples are out fishing. What is noteworthy here is that they have returned to the occupation they held before Jesus's call. Are they simply out for a little rest and relaxation? Or have they, in their amazement and likely bewilderment at the risen Christ, regressed into their prior lives? Perhaps Jesus realizes he needs to refresh his call to them with an appearance over a special beach breakfast. Jesus calls out to them from the shoreline.

Once Peter realizes it is Jesus on the shore, he impulsively leaps out and swims to him. His evident love for Christ is on display as they talk. Jesus thrice asks if Peter loves him—once for each denial—and Peter says yes. Jesus forgives Peter. He then asks Peter to take care of his fledgling church and prophesies about his death for that very church.

Jesus again says to Peter, "Follow me." Peter, however still demonstrates his rashly impulsive side by asking what is to happen to John the disciple. Jesus quickly brings Peter's focus back to his personal mission: "If I want him to remain until I come, what is that to you?" (John 21:23). That is the final time we see Peter act foolishly from a purely human motivation.

Yet, after Peter sees Christ taken up to heaven and is granted (along with the other ten disciples) the Great Commission, Peter is still not the bold evangelist God requires to spread his good news of Christ's kingdom and saving grace. It is the Holy Spirit's arrival that bestows the boldness and wisdom Peter requires to spread this good news.

The Spirit allows Peter to confidently declare to all that Jesus is indeed God's Son who gave himself for the sins of all who believe upon him. After receiving the Spirit, Peter immediately goes outside and explains to the curious crowd that the believers are not drunkards. Then, in a grand, intellectual, and methodic fashion, Peter explains the good news of Jesus using multiple Old Testament passages. He convicts the

Jews for the death of the Messiah. Many repent and ask what they must do to be saved. Peter tells them to repent and be baptized in Christ's name so they can receive forgiveness and the gift of the Holy Spirit.

Peter's message is like any of the Old Testament prophets or John the Baptist: Israel, realize your sin, repent of it, and return to God so that you can reap his blessings.

Peter, the boastful and fiery buffoon, the pridefully outspoken man, is instantly transformed by the Spirit. In Acts, we see Peter convert thousands of Jews in the first few days of his new duties. He preaches unabashedly and without fear in public—even in the temple. He is no longer afraid of anyone or anything. He heals the sick, raises the dead (such as Dorcas or Tabitha in Acts 9), and even confronts the Sanhedrin and other Jewish leaders.

When arrested and confronted, Peter is quick to give the credit for his healing power and bold preaching to Jesus Christ. He strongly affirms there is salvation in none other than him. Peter and John are forbidden by the council to ever teach about or even to speak Jesus's name again. Nevertheless, they retort that they are unable to stop speaking about this truth they have personally seen and heard. They simply must share it!

In Acts 4 and 5, we see that Peter is a mainstay of the administrative issues in the early church. A system of selling, sharing, and distributing funds and goods is established. He is the protagonist in the confrontation with the liars Ananias and Sapphira. He helps set up the deacon system to delegate non-preaching financial matters. Seven holy and wise men, including Stephen, are selected for such tasks so that Peter and the apostles can continue their prayer and preaching ministries.

We are told that believers are increasingly being added to the Lord. The sick are laid out on the streets in the hope that Peter's shadow might fall upon them when he passes. But, although his reputation grows daily, Peter remains humble and no longer boastful. Never again does he act in a proud or rash manner.

He is jailed at least twice more but rescued by angels in dramatic fashion. At least once we are told that he is flogged, to which he rejoices upon being worthy to suffer in the name of Christ.

Peter later meets the converted Saul (now Paul) in Jerusalem. Imagine the meeting of these two wise men of God, both on fire to spread the news of Christ and his plan of salvation. Both men quell the Jews pleading that circumcision and other Old Testament rituals and rules be added to the doctrine of salvation through faith alone by grace alone in Christ alone. Peter is instrumental in keeping the early church together through this major controversy, which could have devastated its unity.

This task is accomplished through a divine vision and confirmed by Peter's visit to a Gentile, the centurion Cornelius. There, Peter sees the Spirit come upon the household, and Peter realizes that God accepts all who fear him and are righteous. He understands that God has no favorites.

Peter then conferences with the Christian leaders in Jerusalem to formally decide on church policy. We are told that he presents a rock-steady and orderly argument for uncomplicated gentile salvation criteria. He discusses his vision and tells how the Spirit came upon Cornelius's family. He leaves no doubt in any mind, and they "praised God, saying, 'So then, even to Gentiles God has granted repentance that leads to life'" (Acts 11:18 NIV).

In Acts 15, the Gentile issue rears its head once more. Judeans begin teaching that circumcision is necessary for salvation. Again, Peters calms the waves. He declares that God makes no distinction between Jew and Gentile. He reiterates that all are saved through the grace of Christ. The assembly assents to his argument (augmented by the accounts of Paul and Barnabas of all God had done on their gentile missions) and drafts a formal letter regarding such. This issue is settled, never to be formally brought up again.

No longer brash and quick-tongued, Peter has embraced and fulfilled his ordained role as a major pillar and administrator of Christ's early church. We see evidence of his ultimate spiritual maturity in his letters, First and Second Peter.

***

Similar to this steadfast rock, this Simon Peter, what does it take for one of us to become a small rock in the foundation of Jesus's kingdom, of which Christ himself is the great rock? We all have specific, individual shortcomings and faults. Our hearts are human. The good Lord knows and understands. Yet, human faults are no excuse to do nothing. He created us to be the person we are for his specific purpose. He uses even our problematic traits to forge us into the instruments he needs. And he does this in our current day just as he did in millennia past.

Consider Peter at his worldly, pre-resurrection level. He probably was not the most fun to be around. I see him in his early years as one of those friends who is entertaining and funny, up to a point. Then, you need a break. It is tiring to be constantly with a loud and proud, impulsive soul. It is, at times, enjoyable and may make you laugh, yet you often feel you need a holiday from the drama. And a blowhard with bravado can sure get you in trouble!

I recall my own friends of Peter's type many years back. While more entertaining than some, as friends go, the drama of having to take care of them (at times literally saving them and me from them) was never fun. Having to keep them from driving while impaired while they insisted they could drive—even physically fighting one for car keys in the mud one night—was less than enjoyable. Or having to pull them from their running vehicle as they lay in it, passed out, foot jammed on the gas but car in park, and having them try to jump out the window as I drove them home, all the while hoping not to have to explain to the police what was happening, are not high points of my younger days.

I, too, remember struggling through a muddy field in a pouring rainstorm to get another friend into his apartment and to bed during the early morning hours. A true miracle occurred as I, fed up, weary, and completely slathered in mud, was about to go out the door. I had left him on his back, unconscious in bed. As the door was closing, I heard a slight gurgle. I went back to check on him. He was profusely vomiting. I was fortunately able to get him on his side immediately so that he did not aspirate. Had I not heard that soft noise, he likely would have expired that day.

Or consider the day I had to talk down the Syracuse football team's entire starting offensive line. It was exciting, certainly, but I did not seek that pleasure ever again. A friend entered his usual Friday night state in which he would drink until he was no longer conscious of his actions yet still able to aggressively function and speak.

A nearby college coed held out her purse toward her boyfriend. My friend rudely and violently slapped it to the ground and gave her a terribly mean look. He then got in the face of her six-foot-seven, three-hundred-fifty-pound boyfriend, who was rightfully coming to her aid and demanding to know why he had done that. My friend was extremely aggressive and posturing. Suddenly, the other four members of that AP top-10 offensive line surrounded us. I tried explaining that he did not know what he was doing, but to them, he appeared to be functioning well. They did not believe me. Fortunately, I was able to talk them down enough for that moment, but they declared they would wait for us outside. Trying to get my friend home a few minutes later, I looked out the front window. Sure enough, there they were: five man-mountains anxiously awaited our presence. Luckily, the place had a back door, so we were able to sneak out and escape despite my friend's protests, "C'mon, man, they're wimps! We can take 'em!" What pure exhilaration.

***

In Simon Peter we see a once-worldly man, with his full arsenal of bravado, pride, and self-initiative, transform into a nearly perfect instrument of God. He is converted from a common, wildly swinging sword slasher into the focused and precise divine blade of his master.

Again, we must ask, how can we achieve a similar transformation in our own modern-day lifetimes? First, we must become selfless. We must realize that our world does not revolve around us. Rather, we must see and bear in mind that our world is God-centered. It serves his purposes, in his timing and in his will. Thus, it exists for his ultimate glory.

Then we must agree to devote ourselves primarily to this great cause. We must deny that which our human hearts relish and yearn for. We need to view our actions and thoughts as part of our Father's grand design. Consider how Christ himself did so. His example is paramount. Attempt to mimic his servanthood. Strive after his ideals. Put yourself second. Then, put yourself one notch lower: below others.

We must then act in God's will, using our divinely granted abilities. Listen for his voice. Time alone spent in communication with him is without comparison. Try it. Ask him, and you shall be enlightened. You will be amazed at what thoughts he plants and what doors he opens within your mind! Become one of your Lord's building blocks, a foundational rock in his continued kingdom building.

Why not do this? We already know which team is the ultimate victor. Yet, his time clock is invisible to us. We do not know which quarter we are in here in our own lives or in this worldly age. We may even be past the fourth quarter's two-minute warning!

Why, then, would you not jump upon his bandwagon as early in its course as possible? Get on board! Enjoy the exciting adventure of playing the game on God's team. You will not be disappointed. Even better, you will not lose.

***

As a final thought, imagine the weeping, post-betrayal Peter. What if he had immediately, then and there, decided to right his mistake: to march back into that courtyard and boldly declare to all present that he was indeed a disciple of Jesus and proclaim him to be their Messiah. What if he explained the many extraordinary deeds he had seen Jesus do and what he had heard him say? Don't you think he would have felt dramatically better? Wouldn't this have been the optimal tonic for his bitter sorrow and deep regret?

Now, let's extrapolate to ourselves. Have you done something that you have extreme and sorrowful regret for? Why let it continue to fester and bother you, affecting your present day as well as the future to come? Even if it has been a long time since the event, isn't there something you can do to right it, now?

XIII. The Woman of God:
Hannah (1 Samuel 1–2)

What is a woman of God? She is one who extols Christlike virtues. If a mother, she impresses these upon her children. If married, she mirrors such in her spouse. We see many examples of such women in Scripture. One of my favorites is Hannah.

We first meet Hannah as 1 Samuel begins. She is one of Elkanah's two wives, and she is childless. Elkanah's other wife, Peninnah, has multiple children.

We are told that Hannah goes yearly with her husband to worship and sacrifice to the Lord at Shiloh. She worships the true God together with her spouse. Praying and worshiping with her husband is certainly one quality of any woman of God. Hannah prays for a son. She also vows to give him to the Lord should her request be granted.

We are given an example of her husband's immense love for her, despite her childlessness. He gives a double portion of sacrificial meat to Hannah. This is more than he gave to his other wife and her children. He also empathizes with her. He discerns her feelings. For example, when her rival taunts her to tears, Elkanah soothes her. He asks why she is troubled, urges her to eat, and suggests that he is better than ten sons for her.

Hannah is never described as being spiteful or vengeful or bitter toward Peninnah. In addition to being respectful to the rival wife, Hannah remains respectful even when Eli the priest accuses her of being drunk while she prays at the tabernacle. Realizing his mistake, a sympathetic Eli asks the Lord to grant her petition for a child, and Hannah's anguished plea is answered by God.

Hers is no mere child. Samuel, her firstborn son, is destined to become the last judge of Israel, a great priest of the Hebrew nation, and a prophet of God.

We then see Hannah's selflessness as well as her gratitude. Both are prominently displayed. Even though Samuel, at that point, is her only child, she takes him to Eli at Shiloh and gives him to the Lord. She states that because God granted her request, she will give her one son up for him and his purposes. Amazingly, she then leaves the child with Eli.

By doing so, Hannah welcomes more scorn and taunting from Peninnah, who likely continued to aggravate Hannah for effectively still having no children. The shame of a childless woman in her village, which Hannah had endured for so long, would also likely come back upon her in some form, especially from those who did not know of her child and his dedication to God.

Hannah's prayer to open 1 Samuel 2 is clearly the worship of a strong and confident woman of the Lord. It is the prayer of one who truly knows who God is. It is the praise of one who rejoices in her salvation through him. She affirms that the Lord is the only God. She mentions that God gives and takes away, both humbling and exalting people. She realizes that God has set the foundations of the earth and that his providence protects his faithful ones while the wicked perish. Her appropriate conception of God's judgment and power are clearly noted here.

Though she gave Samuel up, she still sees her son yearly on her pilgrimage to Shiloh. She makes him robes to wear every year. On these trips, Eli blesses her. She conceives five more children: three boys and two daughters.

***

The name Hannah means grace. She prominently displayed this virtue. She became a mother by her faith in the providence of God. She, no doubt, pleaded for a child for many years before her prayer was answered. While she was certainly sad at times, especially in the face of scorn from others, it never changed her faith. Her conviction was not shaken. She was persistent in her requests and in her worship. She did not become notably frustrated nor did she give up.

How often do we feel unfulfilled or put down or the object of scorn and embarrassment? We all know these feelings. Sometimes they occur quite often. We, unfortunately, cannot control what others think or do. What we must remember, however, is what our loving Father holds us up to be: we are made in the image of his glorious son Jesus!

From the beginning, Hannah had a correct relationship with her husband and with God. While she raised the child Samuel but a short time, she was no doubt a godly mother just as she was a godly wife. And there is little doubt she raised her other five children in the same strong faith that she herself possessed.

A woman of God always reflects the Lord's qualities to those around her. She demonstrates them to her husband, her children, and all who encounter her. She understands her role in the family and makes life easier for all. She does not become angry, vindictive, or cruel, even when criticized. She is not selfish. She gives of herself and her abilities and her time freely. Consider Titus 2:3–5:

> "Older women are to be reverent in behavior, not slanderers, not addicted to much wine. They are to teach what is good, so they may encourage the young women to love their husbands and to love their children, to be self-controlled, pure, homemakers, kind, and submissive to their husbands, so that God's message will not be slandered."

Proverbs 31:10–31 also describes a virtuous and capable wife. She is far more precious than jewels. She is trusted by her husband. She is a hard worker for her household. She is industrious and productive. She helps the poor. She is wise and loving in her instruction. She is not lazy. She fears the Lord and therefore will be praised and rewarded for her labor.

1 Peter 3:3–4 also says, "Your beauty should not come from outward adornment, such as elaborate hairstyles and the wearing of gold jewelry or fine clothes. Rather, it should be that of your inner self, the unfading beauty of a gentle and quiet spirit, which is of great worth in God's sight" (NIV).

Hannah presents a classic example for all Christian women to strive for. While not an easy trail to traverse, hers is the path that will give a woman the most peace as well as the best sense of fulfillment and true joy.

XIV. The Persecuted:
Joseph (Genesis 37–50)

Storms. Tempests. Hurricanes and fires. Such trials will arise in multiples over our lifetimes. Some progress and build slowly, like a gathering thunderstorm rolling in off the plains. Others come on suddenly.

I recall incidents in Alaskan waters where twice I was convinced that we were going to either sink or be thrown up onto a rocky reef and dashed to pieces. These were storms that rolled in off the Bering Sea. Such provided a bit of warning, therefore.

Another time, flying in a small plane over the tall mountains of central Kodiak Island, the sun was out as I viewed the snow-covered peaks below. No oncoming blow was in sight. Now, anyone who pilots small planes knows that Alaska is the most treacherous place to fly. The number of plane crash deaths there exceeds any place elsewhere on our globe. All was going smoothly with the flight. Then, out of nowhere, the plane was struck by a gigantic rogue updraft. It was as if a giant's fist had come up and punched the bottom of the plane. It went way up, then dove down rapidly as the pilot desperately tried to regain control. Shaken, we fortunately were able to pull out of the gust's icy grasp.

A further time, living in extremely dry West Texas (where we once even went one full year without any rain whatsoever), I was driving to work in the early morning darkness to make my 5 a.m. hospital rounds. The road dropped steeply as it went down into an arroyo. This wash was typically a dry drainage. Yet, it could be dangerous when it channeled flood waters into very high currents. While rare, that sort of thing occasionally happened from rainstorms that occurred ten to twenty miles away. In those cases, there was no warning.

That morning, it had rained a good deal overnight farther up north, and the rushing waters now filled the arroyo to a five-foot depth. Driving quickly down the hill as I usually did, I saw the flowing water in my headlights but was unable to stop. All I could do was floor it and try to get through to the opposite side. Water lifted my truck. Floating freely, it pushed me to the left. As I looked that way, I saw three vehicles already piled on top of each other just twenty yards away. But my truck had also moved forward in the current as well as to the side, and, miraculously, its front wheels touched dry pavement on the opposite side of the flood. Thus, I was able to continue up the hill and out of harm's way.

Another roadway incident occurred in the same West Texas town on an expressway's elevated loop. This was a single lane with minimal shoulders, basically a sharply curving narrow bridge without much visibility. Driving in to see a subarachnoid hemorrhage in critical condition early one dark winter morning, I did not see the black ice. My truck spun out. My front end plowed into the concrete wall of the narrow single lane, and it almost wedged in sideways! Jumping out, I saw the metal of the fender was pushed in against the wheel, so I could not drive it off. It was a blessing that it was early morning with sparse traffic. Still, anyone coming around that curve would have a blind eye to what was happening until right on top of me. With that ice, they would not be able to stop. I also had nowhere to run besides either getting far away from my vehicle (which I immediately considered) or jumping down onto the interstate below, which was an even less favorable option. Watching for lights, I grabbed my tire iron and (using unusual strength from the adrenaline, I presume, with perhaps a divine assist as well) pried back the fender from the wheel. My truck could now turn and roll, although I still only had several feet to either side of the vehicle. So, I had to back up and go forward multiple times before I could get it headed in the correct direction. Miraculously, I was able to get off that ramp before any unsuspecting vehicle came flying around at the sixty-five-mile-an-hour speed limit. Such would have been disastrous for both of us. Fortunately, it did not come to such.

Yet, Christians who are persecuted for their beliefs exist in much more extreme circumstances than these. I address this at length in *Rise and Soar*. I know Christian brothers and sisters who have left homelands to minister to these persecuted souls. I also know several people who have been persecuted themselves from lands like Eritrea, Tanzania, Nigeria, the Philippines, India, Turkey, and North Korea. Some lost family and friends to the persecution. Others are imprisoned or being hunted as I write. They run underground churches, smuggle Bibles across borders, and hold secret meetings and Scripture studies.

The question is not whether they are going to be caught. The question is when. What always floors me is what many of them so selflessly say: "We consider it our training to do these activities. Our mission begins once we are caught." By this they mean they can then witness for Christ to their persecutors and to fellow prisoners. How hard it is for us in the West to understand the great sacrifices they readily make for God's kingdom! Talk about trailblazers for our Lord!

Trials, accidents, storms, and persecutions abound in this life. They threaten to sweep us away. Some give us fair warning. Others do not. There is no escaping them. We must all go through them. And they come with positive and negative outcomes. Have you ever considered it may be the response (which emanates from the attitude a person takes) while within these tempests that determines whether there will be overwhelmingly positive results?

***

Consider the example of Joseph. Jacob's favorite son Joseph is the blatant recipient of fatherly favoritism. Jacob gives Joseph a brilliant and regal robe that clearly elevates him to a place of preference among his ten siblings. His brothers see that their father loves Joseph more than them. This fuels a growing hatred toward their younger sibling. We are told they cannot even speak to him peacefully.

Joseph then fans the fire by telling his brothers about a dream in which they bow down to him in deference, perhaps even in worship or servanthood. He further intensifies their hatred by telling them about a second dream in which he is elevated above them all. At this point, his father, Jacob, does step in, but it is too late. Jacob's lack of appropriate fatherly insight and intervention early on has already ignited a devastating cascade of unstoppable events.

The brothers are so angry that one day they plot to kill Joseph in the fields. Joseph had been at home rather than helping with the flocks. But Jacob sends him to give a message to his brothers. (Joseph appears to have had a privileged place in the family, and at least at this time, he was not required to perform the common herding labors that his ten older brothers were responsible for.) Fortunately, Joseph's eldest brother, Reuben, convinces them to spare his life. Reuben plans to rescue him later. Judah then suggests selling Joseph to a passing caravan. He is sold for twenty pieces of silver as a slave and is taken to Egypt. The brothers slather goat's blood on the robe and tell Jacob a wild animal killed his favored son.

In Egypt, Joseph is sold to Potiphar, a high-ranking officer who is captain of Pharaoh's guard. It is clear to all that the Lord is with Joseph. He becomes successful at all he endeavors while serving in his master's household. He becomes Potiphar's personal attendant. Potiphar puts him in charge of the entire household and of all that he owns. Genesis 39 describes how the Lord poured out his blessings upon the house because of Joseph.

His master has no worries for a time, until Joseph's good looks attract Potiphar's wife. Joseph refuses to sleep with her, but she continues her attempts to seduce him. One day she grabs his robe and insists, but Joseph breaks free and runs outside. Still holding his coat, she accuses Joseph of attempted rape. Potiphar unfortunately is blind to the truth, and Joseph is imprisoned.

The jailer realizes how blessed Joseph is—even in prison. Joseph is made responsible for all that occurs there. He is given authority over all prisoners. In the dungeon, God makes all Joseph's efforts successful. Yet, we see that early in his imprisonment, Joseph still makes excuses and feels unjustly wronged twice over: "Get me out of this prison. For I was kidnapped from the land of the Hebrews, and even here I have done nothing that they should put me in the dungeon" (Genesis 40:14b–15).

While imprisoned, Joseph correctly interprets the dreams of two fellow prisoners. He is nevertheless forgotten in prison for two more years. But when Pharaoh has dreams none of his men can discern, the cupbearer, who had been in prison with Joseph, finally recalls him. Joseph tells Pharaoh his dreams mean there will be seven years of plenty followed by seven years of severe famine. Now, having had an appropriate adjustment of his attitude, Joseph gives God the glory. He tells Pharaoh that he himself is unable to interpret dreams and that God is the actual translator. He says God is warning Egypt about what is to occur so that the famine's devastation can be minimized.

This shows Joseph's new confidence. He trusts God through all that happens. He is no longer whining and feeling that he has been unfairly treated. And he is thus rewarded with showers of blessings!

Further, Pharaoh also realizes that God is with Joseph. He clearly sees that this ex-convict is the optimal man needed to oversee the food storage and distribution plans. He places this ex-prisoner slave in charge of the entire Egyptian empire. Joseph is second-in-command, only outranked by Pharaoh himself. He is given an Egyptian wife and is soon riding in the second chariot just behind Pharaoh. The command "Abrek!" is shouted as he proceeds, which means kneel. What a reversal God has orchestrated!

And as we would expect, with his focus remaining upon God, all that Joseph attempts meets with success. He stores up foodstuffs beyond measure. And he is granted two sons.

When the famine arrives, no nation is secure except the land of Egypt. Egypt becomes the provider for the entire region, including Canaan. From there, Jacob sends Joseph's ten older brothers (excluding the youngest, Benjamin) to Egypt to buy grain.

Joseph recognizes them, but they do not realize it is him. He is at first harsh with them. He accuses them of spying. He imprisons Simeon and instructs the others to take food back home. Joseph also commands them to return to Egypt and bring Benjamin with them.

The distance from Egypt to Canaan is about five hundred miles. The trip with heavily laden donkeys likely took three to four weeks. Imagine the brothers' guilt, regret, and fear on their journey. And imagine how reluctantly they told their aging father the news about Benjamin. They must have feared that such a request might overwhelm him. And when they saw the money they used to pay for the grain was still in their sacks, how much more were they afraid!

Jacob flatly refuses to let them return with Benjamin—in effect giving up his son Simeon. But once the food runs out, Jacob assents to the return journey, accompanied by Benjamin, gifts, and twice the sum of the returned money.

Joseph meets Benjamin and dines with his brothers. Then once more, he sends them home with the food and their money. He also puts his silver cup into Benjamin's bag. Benjamin, later caught with the cup, is accused of the theft. He is designated to become Joseph's slave. But his brother Judah offers himself instead to spare Jacob the anguish.

At this gesture, Joseph finally reveals his identity. He explains that God was at work through their sin and turned their evil to good. And he invites their entire nation to emigrate to Egypt. Pharaoh himself warmly welcomes them. He gifts them land and goods, saying, "The best of all the land of Egypt is yours" (Genesis 45:20b).

So, Joseph joyously reunites with his father, and the Hebrews are established into an initially high place in Goshen, the best grazing land of Egypt. Jacob dies soon thereafter and is brought back to Canaan for burial. Joseph's brothers then fear he may now become vengeful, but Joseph reassures them. He promises to take care of them, explaining again how God used their intended evil actions for the good of the entire Israelite nation. Joseph finally has his attitude and perception in order.

***

Why do bad things happen to us? Why is there evil in our world? We are good, or at least we try our best to be good people. Why must we and the whole world be subject to calamities and tragedies? [3]

People respond to bad things in three different ways. Some regress and recede into their shells. They become hardened and cold to everything, including themselves and those close to them and others in the world at large. By doing so, they rob themselves of their joy. It becomes hard to see joy or good in anything. These people become highly suspicious and persistently cynical, embittered souls.

A second group is more extroverted. They complain and whine and blame everything and everyone else. They always cry foul and believe they are unfairly oppressed and suffering great injustices. They fail to look to a solution. They do not accept any responsibility. They do not see that God is present even within such circumstances. They do not mentally go a step further to spiritually realize that their heavenly Father is working all for their ultimate benefit.

When we first meet Joseph, he is spiritually established within this second group. Yet, at some point during his imprisonment, he changes his attitude. He enters the third group of responders.

The third response people can have to difficulties, storms, trials, and evils is a positive one. No, they are not overjoyed to be within the tempest. But they keep in the forefront of their minds that there absolutely is a reason, some purpose, for that storm encircling them. They stop making excuses. They accept their current reality, realizing it is not permanent. And they recognize that God is using bad circumstances to forge them into his finely tuned instrument.

The imprisoned Joseph must have looked back at his boastful, mouthy youth with regret. His attitude and actions irritated not only his ten older brothers but his father, Jacob, as well. He was plainly privileged by his father, and Joseph chose to accept this role. He does not seem to have carried his share of the family's livestock duties. This undoubtedly caused him to lose the respect of his brothers as much as his bravado did.

A bit of insight and empathy would have gone a long way to minimize the tension in the tents of Israel and his kinfolk. But, following his father's suboptimal example, Joseph lacked those qualities as well. He did not perceive or care about his brothers' feelings. As a result, they plotted against him, and he was ultimately eliminated from their lives and his country of birth.

Yet, once Joseph adopted the appropriate attitude and realized that God should receive his primary focus, the blessings began to flow. We are not told exactly how long this took. It appears to have been more than two years at least. Our Lord's timing is not our own.

Nonetheless, Joseph is ultimately rescued. Within a single day's time, he is released, cleans up, and becomes the second most powerful man in the entire Egyptian empire! That certainly was worth waiting for!

Had he not been sold and imprisoned, the greater good would not have occurred. God used bad things to work for the ultimate benefit of multitudes. And not just in Joseph's lifetime: those benefits continued into the time of Christ. They set the stage for his entry into our world as God incarnate so that all could be redeemed. And the benefits yet continue into our modern era today.

The lesson here is that you must not give up. Keep your focus fixed on God. Pray and commune with him in prayer and in his holy Word. The showers of blessings are coming, but only he knows when. Giving up and throwing in the towel should never be your alternative. By doing so, you may well miss his reward in your life! Stay your course with God as your pilot. It can be hard to see him, but he is right there in that mess with you!

XV. The Lying and Scheming Cheater:
Jacob (Genesis 25–50)

We all know people who plot and scheme—people who lie and cheat to get ahead. These are selfish people. They look out for themselves primarily. They, without concern, will trod on the hopes, possessions, and even the dreams of others if doing so will benefit themselves. These are people who doggedly climb the ladder of success no matter whom or what they step upon to get there. The end goal of their self-advancement is more important than anything else. Friendships, family relationships, the feelings of others, and what is right and fair are thrown completely out the window.

Unfortunately, we all have this tendency in our hearts. In some of us, it is satisfactorily subdued. In others, such as Jacob, it is quite overt. This type of obviously self-motivated person, once their tendency becomes clear, often causes others to dissociate from him.

Let us look at the story of Jacob in Genesis. Jacob is born as the second of twins, grasping his brother Esau's heel as he enters the world closely behind him. Throughout his young life, Jacob daily contemplates his dire predicament. He knows he does not have the birthright accredited to the firstborn and thus will never achieve the prominence in the family he so desires.

His twin Esau, however, has little concern for his birthright. Perhaps this is because he knows it is already his. He spends his time away from people in the fields hunting. Jacob is a quiet man who stays at home. He is loved best by his mother, Rebekah, while his father, Isaac, loves Esau best.

There is a problem with the twins' upbringing. Their parents clearly allow favoritism to be displayed within the family. As we have seen in other stories, and as occurs in modern life, allowing favoritism can produce exceedingly bad results down the road.

Jacob seizes his opportunity one day when Esau comes in famished from the field. Esau asks for the bread and soup Jacob is cooking. Jacob first asks for his birthright in return, which Esau readily gives up. He swears to Jacob that he is indeed selling his birthright to him. Esau despises his birthright and trades it for a mere pittance.

Later, a debilitated Isaac with poor vision calls Esau to get him some game from the field. His father asks him to prepare a meal so that he can bless him with his birthright before Isaac passes. Rebekah overhears this and tells Jacob. Jacob garbs in goat skin as his mother cooks a meal she knows Isaac will love. She has Jacob take it to Isaac, his arms and neck covered with the goat hair to resemble Esau's.

As Jacob brings Isaac the food, his father is suspicious given the speed with which it was produced. Isaac also recognizes Jacob's voice. Yet, when he touches him, the rough hairy skin fools him. Twice he asks whom Jacob is. Twice Jacob lies, proclaiming himself to be Esau the firstborn.

After eating the misrepresented meal, Isaac pronounces his blessing upon Jacob. Esau brings his meal soon after, and he and Isaac realize they have been duped. Isaac tells Esau that he cannot give another blessing. He tells Esau that he has made Jacob master over him, then flatly states that he can do nothing else for him. He reiterates that Esau must serve his brother Jacob. This stirs great anger in Esau, who plans to kill Jacob.

Rebekah gets to Jacob first and urges him to flee to his uncle Laban in Haran. Before he leaves, his parents urge him to take a wife from one of his cousins in Haran rather than a Canaanite. Isaac again blesses Jacob on his departure, extending God's blessing of Abraham onto him.

On his journey, Jacob has a dream in which Yahweh presents himself and promises to give Jacob the territory he is in. He promises, as he did to Abraham, that Jacob's descendants will be a great people who will bless the earth. God reassures Jacob he will be with him wherever he goes. He promises that he shall bring him back to this land and that he will never leave him. Upon awakening from the dream, Jacob promises that if God will remain with and help him on the journey, ultimately allowing him to return safely to home, the Lord would then be his God. He also promises to give 10 percent of all that is given to him as an offering back to God.

In Haran, Jacob meets Laban's daughter Rachel and falls in love with her. He promises his uncle that he will work seven years to earn her hand in marriage. Laban, however, deceives Jacob, turning the tables on the master deceiver himself. He performs a wedding night switch in which he places his older daughter, Leah, into Jacob's tent instead of Rachel.

In the morning, Jacob realizes he has been deceived. His uncle asks for seven more years' work for Rachel. Jacob complies. He ultimately marries Rachel as well.

Unfortunately, we soon see more family drama. We are told that Jacob loves Rachel noticeably more. Nevertheless, Rachel is not able to conceive. Leah does conceive. She bears Reuben, then Simeon, followed by Levi, and finally, Judah.

At this point, Rachel, upset at being barren, demands sons from Jacob. She gives him her slave Bilhah as a third wife. Bilhah bears two sons, Dan and then Naphtali. Leah has stopped having children, so she throws yet another woman into the mix. She gives her slave Zilpah to Jacob as a fourth wife. Zilpah then gives birth to Gad and Asher.

The psychosocial drama continues. Leah buys Jacob for intercourse one night by giving Rachel some mandrakes. She then bears a fifth son, Issachar. She later conceives Zebulun as well as a daughter named Dinah. Rachel then finally conceives and gives birth to Joseph.

In the meantime, despite the four-wife home tent, Jacob is becoming successful. He desires to return to his homeland. Yet, Laban asks him to stay. In return, Jacob asks that all Laban's speckled, spotted, and dark-colored sheep and goats be given to him as wages. Laban agrees and removes all such animals from his flocks. Jacob then practices more deception. He places tree branches in the water troughs, which he knows will breed future lambs and kid goats that are streaked, speckled, and spotted in color. And he does so when the stronger, better sheep are breeding. Jacob knows these will produce quality offspring. He does not put out the branches for the genetically weaker sheep and goats. So, in time, Jacob's breeding evolves much better flocks than his uncle's. We are told that Jacob becomes very rich, having many flocks, slaves, camels, and donkeys. Understandably, Laban and his clan are now upset with Jacob. They realize he has deceitfully built his wealth from theirs. God then comes to Jacob and tells him to return to his homeland.

Once more, Laban is deceived by Jacob. Jacob does not tell his uncle-now-father-in-law he is leaving. He sneaks out of town with all he has. To show how the lack of authority and deceit is spreading, Rachel even steals her father's household idols. Laban pursues and catches up to them. God, however, warns Laban against any aggression toward Jacob. Jacob's excuse to Laban is that he was afraid. Yet, Jacob had just reassured his wives that God was with him and therefore they could not be harmed.

Jacob then begins a tirade against Laban. He repeatedly cites his hard work for Laban and Laban's unfair treatment of him. He declares how hard the past twenty years were working for his uncle in the heat and cold. Laban and Jacob then make a covenant between them, and they part in peace.

The next great concern for Jacob is seeing his brother, Esau, upon returning home. This is understandable, as Esau had previously been so incensed that he had threatened to kill Jacob. Although it has been twenty years, Jacob knows Esau to be a fiery and lion-like strongman. Certainly, his anger is something to be feared.

Always thinking of self-preservation, Jacob sends messengers ahead of him. When told that Esau is coming with four hundred men, Jacob is extremely frightened. He splits his camp into two groups. He asks for God's rescue, reminding God of his promises to protect and to prosper him. He prepares an extensive gift of livestock for Esau, then sends his servants ahead of him with the herds.

Jacob, meanwhile, crosses a stream and takes up a strategic position with his wives and eleven sons. From here, he might have a chance to escape if the scouts he sent ahead to meet Esau are greeted with his wrath.

That night, a man comes into camp and wrestles with Jacob until dawn. In the morning, he strikes and dislocates Jacob's hip. Then the man, who is the angel of the Lord, renames Jacob. Jacob is called Israel from then on.

The next day, Jacob sees Esau and his men approaching. He strategically puts his female slaves and their children first, followed by Leah and her children, and, lastly, he positions Rachel and Joseph into the safest zone. He is protecting his best-loved family members as much as he can. He then goes ahead and is greeted warmly by Esau. Esau first declines but then, after being urged, accepts Jacob's gifts. Esau then asks Jacob to follow him home to Seir, but Jacob declines. He tells Esau to go ahead while he continues more slowly, citing as an excuse the many children and livestock he has. He tells Esau he will meet him at Seir. He further turns down Esau's request to leave some of his men there. Esau returns to his home, but Jacob does not follow. Contrary to his statement, he instead goes to Succoth. There, his true intent is declared as he builds himself a house. He even constructs stalls for his livestock. He buys land and sets up an altar to God. These are certainly not the actions of a man who plans to move onward anytime soon. Jacob still appears to fear his twin brother. He thus continues calculating and scheming, always thinking of the best way to protect himself.

Jacob is also indecisive regarding other family matters. He does not act in response to the rape of his daughter, Dinah, by a pagan Hivite prince. He delays because his sons are not with him. When they return, his sons, not Jacob, hatch a plan to avenge their sister. They tell the men of the city they must be circumcised if they are to live together. So, all the pagans are circumcised. Jacob's sons then kill all the males in the city while they are recovering from their wounds and plunder it. Jacob is upset. He says they have made him look bad to the nations of Canaan.

He is fearful that they will attack and destroy his family in return. He again seems to have forgotten the promises God made to give him the land and to be with and protect him. He appears to worry much more about his reputation and safety than he does about his daughter.

God then tells Jacob to settle in Bethel and build an altar to the Lord. Jacob finally begins to wise up. He tells his family to get rid of all their idols and to purify themselves. He realizes God has helped him through his trials and has been constantly with him, providing for him and keeping him safe. He is finally developing a firm confidence in the Lord rather than being so fearful. He no longer feels he must constantly connive and scheme to protect himself and what is his.

At Bethel, God again blesses Jacob. He reiterates the promise he made to Abraham: that Israel will inherit the land, that God will bless him, and that he will have many descendants.

Rachel then dies during the birth of Jacob's youngest son, Benjamin.

Jacob sees his father, Isaac, once more before Isaac expires. Jacob then stays in Canaan. However, family problems continue. As we saw above, Jacob overtly displays favoritism to his son Joseph, causing Joseph's older brothers to hate their sibling so greatly they plot to kill him, but eventually sell him into slavery. Yet, as we saw in the story of Joseph, this was ultimately a very good thing that God deemed necessary for the benefit of the Israelite nation. Jacob's ten older sons, having learned from his example, deceive their father by giving him Joseph's bloodied robe. Jacob believes a wild animal has killed Joseph, and his sons do not correct him or tell him that Joseph is still alive.

Years later, during the severe famine, Jacob sends his ten older sons to Egypt to buy grain. Yet fearful, he does not allow Benjamin to accompany them. He fears that something might happen to his youngest child born of his beloved wife, Rachel. When nine of his sons return (minus Simeon, who is held by the undercover and unrecognized Joseph in Egypt), Jacob whines about having to take Benjamin to Egypt, exclaiming, "Everything happens to me!"

By refusing to let Benjamin go to Egypt, Jacob, in effect, gives up Simeon. He writes one son off to avoid the possibility of losing his favorite.

Ultimately, though, with the famine persisting, the clan needs to return to Egypt for more food. Jacob continues to whine and point fingers. He asks his sons why they told the Egyptian nobleman that they had another brother. Finally, Jacob agrees to allow Benjamin to return to Egypt with them—but only because the entire family is at risk of starvation. Still a schemer, Jacob sends a magnificent gift of balsam, honey, gum and rosin, pistachios, and almonds and tells them to take twice as much money with them.

As we know, all goes well on the return trip to Egypt. Joseph reveals his identity to his brothers, and they return to get Jacob and bring him to Egypt also. Liars, however, have a hard time believing others. When his sons tell him Joseph is still alive, Jacob does not believe them. However, he is then revived in spirit and sets out for Egypt. God reassures him in a dream, telling him not to be afraid to go. He promises to continue to make Israel a great nation. He promises to be with Israel while there and to one day bring Israel back to their homeland.

Jacob is overjoyed to see Joseph again. The Israelites settle in the fertile Goshen region of Egypt to raise their livestock. Jacob then meets and blesses Pharaoh.

A dwindling Jacob later makes Joseph vow to bury him in Canaan rather than Egypt upon his death. Jacob's last recorded words are blessings to each of his sons, the men destined to become the twelve tribes of Israel. He foretells specific things that will happen to each of them. He again commands that he be buried in Canaan with Abraham, Sarah, Isaac, Rebekah, and Leah. Following his death, Jacob's family fulfills his burial request.

***

We see several common recurrences in this long story about Jacob. His very name means cheater. He is constantly thinking of ways to preserve and better himself, the most-loved persons in his family, and his possessions. Thus, he does not appear to have true peace of mind or heart.

Yet, God himself repeatedly and even physically appears to him. God promises to be with Jacob and to prosper him, to make him into a great nation, and to never leave him. Still, Jacob often seems to forget and to doubt this. This results in conniving, scheming, and lying, that is, a general attitude and practice of routine deception. Jacob is not a character who would be trusted by those closest to him.

Anyone who acts like Jacob needs to change their attitude. This type of person needs to shift from their self-view to a God-oriented worldview. If you are a Jacob, let me say this: no matter how driven you are, there is only so far that self-motivation will get you in this world. You will never have true peace. You will never perceive adequate fulfillment. You will always be reaching for more, anxious about loss or injury, pointing out the unfairness in the world, perhaps even whining that your existence is miserable. You will never have true joy.

Alternatively, when you possess a God-centered view of the world, you realize you are not the epicenter. Rather, you see you are part of the pathway to God's kingdom. You understand that you can, with satisfaction and fulfillment, guide not only yourself but others to him. This creates an exciting life-adventure. It also brings you peace of heart and mind, as you realize God is indeed in control. He is with you. Nothing can harm you. His plan is firmly in place for you. He will never leave nor forsake you. This results in a true joy throughout your lifetime, until you are taken up to infinite joy and eternal paradise with your heavenly Father.

Yet, how hard it is to adopt this mindset. And how much harder it is to persist in it, day in and day out, especially when the storms of this crazy life swoop in off the horizon. The optimal way to achieve this perspective is to gain progressive confidence in the Lord as your life evolves. Look back over your lifetime and see what examples of goodness God has accomplished so far in bringing you to this very point. Meet with him daily in prayer and in his holy Word. Pray before you read and ask him what you need to understand today. Then, take time to listen. He will speak to you. He will reassure you. You will realize he is always with you! You will then feel little need to cheat, to scheme, to connive, or to lie. He will change your heart!

XVI. The Wise and Determined Builder: Nehemiah

My daughter and I had just built a life-sized X-wing fighter out of a huge fallen tree. We burned out its cockpit, put in an instrument panel, then attached wings and cannons. We painted it the classic orange and white. We attached multiple engine parts, emptying ten wheelbarrows full of garage odds and ends, including a roof vent as a revolving R2-D2. We had a lot of fun working on this project together (with many teaching moments too). And that ten-year-old loved it!

Her next declared goal—with only two months until the day she planned to have a Star Wars birthday party for her friends—was for us to construct a life-sized Ewok village complete with multiple levels of platforms, steps, and climbing ropes up in the trees behind our home. Even my wife predicted that there was "no way we would finish in time."

Soon thereafter, we gathered all the scrap lumber around the house and garage and headed into the woods to look at the site. We were able to frame three levels, slowly envisioning the completed project. Then we ran out of wood. Doesn't it always seem that despite what looks to be appropriate supplies, more is inevitably needed no matter the project?

Time was of the essence, as was money. I estimated it would take about $3,000 of additional wood to complete a project of this size. Our thoughts and visions had been bigger than our supplies and finances.

Nevertheless, we were blessed by new construction sites of several nearby houses where workers threw scrap lumber nightly into their on-site dumpsters. Yes, these were full of nails, bowed, broken, cut into. They were poor pieces of wood for building a home, but for us, these dumpsters were treasure troves. Yes, we were cut with nails and screws. We received many splinters and bruises. Yet, we brought home truckload after truckload of castaway wood. While it was tempting to grab a few of the new boards lying nearby, we never did. In the end, we were able to obtain all the lumber needed for the project without spending a dime! And with just three days to spare before her birthday, we finished the project on a sunny Halloween afternoon. God had certainly provided, despite our initial poor planning!

***

In our lives, we have all known examples of wise businesspeople, and we have known people who blindly rushed into a project without appropriate resources or alternative courses of action. Nehemiah's is the story of a model businessperson with a grand vision of his goal, one he did not blindly rush into. He calculated. He planned. He took his time even when he had been granted royal authority and possessed the means to complete his project. He still did not rush into his vision proudly, loudly, nor boastfully.

Nehemiah is a man in exile, and he is Persian king Artaxerxes's wine taster. He is trustworthy enough to have attained this role. Yet, we first meet Nehemiah in a very saddened state. He tells the king that he is depressed because his home city of Jerusalem lies destroyed.

The king grants his request to return and rebuild the city and its wall. He writes letters to grant Nehemiah safe passage. He provides timber for the gates, the walls, and the homes that are to be rebuilt. The king even sends foot soldiers and cavalry with Nehemiah for safety on the journey.

On his return to Jerusalem, local people hostile to Israel become upset at this plan of restoration and assistance to the Hebrews. Wisely, Nehemiah first goes out at night to assess the scene without telling anyone his plans. Then, he announces to the Israelites that they should rebuild Jerusalem, and he encourages them into action.

Israel's enemies mock and despise them. They threaten Nehemiah. Yet, the rebuilding continues. One by one, they rebuild the gates. They raise the walls. We are told that women help alongside the men. It is a grand and inspired effort as the city gradually comes back together. Many different hands contribute, a testament to the power of a grand motive or principle.

As the work progresses, their enemies' derision turns to anger. Sanballat, an enemy leader, doubts and ridicules their success. Nevertheless, the work continues. The wall is halfway to its prior height. The enemies plot to fight against Jerusalem to confuse and hinder their efforts.

Nehemiah then wisely stations guards twenty-four hours per day. Armed men protect the working families. This encourages the people, taking away their fear. Nehemiah grandly inspires them as well:

"Remember the great and awe-inspiring Lord, and fight for your countrymen, your sons and daughters, your wives and homes" (Nehemiah 4:14).

Laborers work with one hand and hold a weapon in the other. Builders have swords on their waists. Nehemiah has a trumpeter ready to rally the men to wherever attacks may come. He encourages them by saying, "Our God will fight for us!" (Nehemiah 4:20).

Nehemiah as governor of Judah is a good ruler. He takes on and corrects the Hebrews' social and economic issues in accordance with the Law. Prior governors taxed and took provisions from their people. Nehemiah refuses to do anything of the sort. He knows how poverty-stricken and demoralized the common people are. Yet, Jewish nobles are taxing and enslaving their fellow Israelites. He pleads with them to stop charging interest and return fields, vineyards, olive groves, and houses to rightful owners. He tells them to stop enslaving their own people. By shaming these noblemen, Nehemiah rapidly accomplishes what is necessary without conflict or argument.

Nehemiah's wisdom is evident once more when Sanballat, Tobiah, and Geshem, the enemy leaders, ask him to a meeting outside of Jerusalem. Realizing they plan to kill him, he refuses. Five separate requests for this conference are made, yet Nehemiah wisely defers.

Their enemies then imply that the Jews plan to rebel. They threaten to tell the king that there will be treason and revolution. They state that they believe Nehemiah will proclaim himself king of Judah. Nehemiah soundly denies it and asks God to strengthen him. He does not give in to their intimidation attempts.

Amazingly, the wall is completed in fifty-two days. Only a few people live inside the city, so Nehemiah smartly posts appropriate guards. Many of the exiles then return from Babylon, and Nehemiah registers them all by genealogy. Their enemies then lose all confidence because they realize this has only been accomplished through the hand of God.

Nehemiah then gathers the people. He has Ezra the scribe read the Law to them. Ezra reads from daybreak until noon. The Lord is worshiped, and his laws are explained to the populace. The people have a great celebration. Significantly, we are told that they understand what is read to them. This is extremely important. Nehemiah is not only rebuilding the physical city, but he is also implanting the moral and holy laws of God within the people's hearts and minds. He understands that both aspects are important: both the physical and the spiritual needs of his nation.

Further, the Jews celebrate the Festival of Booths for the first time since the days of Joshua son of Nun. They confess their sins with fasting, wearing of sackcloth, and putting dust on their heads. All praise the Lord for his providence, his promises, and their deliverance throughout the ages.

Israel then makes a vow of faithfulness, promising with a sworn oath to obey God's laws as given through Moses. They vow not to intermarry with the pagans around them. They also agree not to buy or sell or conduct any other type of business on the Sabbath. Further, they agree to leave the land uncultivated and cancel every debt each seventh year, per God's Year of Jubilee command. They also promise sufficient tithes and offerings to provide adequate care for God's house and his priests.

Nehemiah organizes a dedication ceremony for the wall. It is a grand celebration of worship and thanksgiving. Music and singing are prominent. There is great rejoicing because God has finally given them rescue and security. The Lord has returned them to the land he had promised long ago.

Nehemiah makes further reforms as well. After going back to King Artaxerxes in Babylon, he returns to Jerusalem to find Tobiah the Ammonite breaking Moses's law against pagans entering the house of God. Tobiah has been given lodging in the temple. Nehemiah throws him and all his possessions out and purifies the rooms. He also finds that the Levites are not being appropriately provided for, so they have gone back to working their fields to feed themselves. He corrects each of these matters.

He also sees people breaking the Sabbath. Some press grapes and others conduct business upon the holy day. He orders the city gates closed on the night before the Sabbath. They are not to be reopened until the Sabbath is completed. He also finds Jews who have intermarried with local pagans. He rebukes them as well, cursing them, beating some of the men, and even pulling out their hair. He reminds them of their oath about not intermarrying and makes them retake it. He insightfully reminds them of how even wise Solomon became entrapped in sin by marrying pagan idol worshipers. Nehemiah in summary reviews all God's rules and laws once again, doing his best to keep the people on a straight path.

***

The thirteen chapters of this brief book reveal a remarkable character: Nehemiah. He is a wise and holy man. His heart is for God. He does not think about himself. He truly desires for God to be glorified as well as to help others, especially the impoverished and downtrodden, the abused, and those unfairly taken advantage of.

These character traits are exactly why Nehemiah is so grieved by the thought of the holy city in ruins with its population scattered and unprotected. By being politely humble yet also stepping out and asking Artaxerxes for the opportunity to rebuild the city, he displays full confidence in the Lord. He is not afraid of rebuttal, penalty, or torture.

Nehemiah then, when given permission, materials, and men, promptly sets out to complete the project. And this he does very wisely. He provides appropriate protection for the workers so that no tragedies from foreign attackers can occur. Once the wall is built, he re-educates the people on the laws of God so they could live wisely again as God's chosen people. His reforms and re-education are critical, as many of these rules were not being practiced. Many had even been forgotten over the centuries since Joshua succeeded Moses. Yet, true to form, after visiting Babylon and later returning to Jerusalem, Nehemiah sees that the people are still not following many of the vows they have made to the Lord. He once again corrects and sets them on the appropriate path.

Nehemiah was a valiant and tireless trailblazer for his Lord God. Consider Nehemiah's overwhelming task. His people could easily have become discouraged when they saw the large amount of work to be done. We get discouraged too when we see a yard completely overgrown after days or weeks of rain have not allowed us to tend to it or after we come back from a prolonged vacation. Or when a simple paint job becomes endless replacement and staging work as rotted timbers are discovered in the wall or window frames. Sometimes the work seems overwhelming!

Imagine how much more overwhelming it appeared to the Israelites. They clearly saw the blackened stones and the destroyed city wall and houses. Certainly, Nehemiah is a grand encourager. He is a master cheerleader and speech-giver. He would have made Vince Lombardi, General George Patton, and Sir Winston Churchill proud. He knows how to stir his people into appropriate action. And once he does so, with the hand of the Lord working through them, the people begin to see progress. At that point, it certainly became much easier for them to continue their labors. Seeing progress as we work, even though more daunting tasks lie ahead, propels us forward with excitement. It motivates us.

Nehemiah does not back down. He remains encouraged and positive. And he does so despite opposition, intimidation, problems with his own countrymen, and ignorance by many of the Israelites of appropriate conduct. He does his very best. And with the Lord's help, he confronts and corrects each issue as it arises.

Nehemiah is truly a master of multiple things, not only of physical architecture. He is also a spiritual architect, forming the Israelite nation into a people who would glorify God by following his laws and commands.

How can we be a wise, valiant, and inspiring trailblazer such as Nehemiah? We first need to assume an attitude of confidence, knowing that our Lord is ever with us. We also must be certain that we are following his will and keeping his holy commandments. We should encourage others, even when we meet with disappointment, frustration, intimidation, or outright assault. And when God blesses us, we must remember to remain humble and give him the glory.

As with Nehemiah, our progress will never be steadily upward without problems and issues arising. What we must keep in the forefront of our mind is that no matter what issue or storm arises, we still have the ability, with our Lord's assistance, to tackle all such challenges. In this story, even though work needed to slow down due to outside threats and infighting within the Israelite community, the project still progressed. It never came to a complete halt. We similarly must not worry about the size of the task. We likewise are not to be discouraged when people tell us what we are doing is useless, that it is too grand of a plan, it will never work, or that we are not qualified to accomplish such. Physical threats and intimidation, internal strife, or even the seeming impossibility of the task can loom as daunting mountains before us, obstacles that seek to diminish our drive and reduce our spirit.

Ridicule, scorn, embarrassment, and abuse may well have already affected your own life's goals and plans. Have you ever launched into something, putting your heart, mind, soul, and resources fully toward such effort, but then ridicule or staunch opposition rises against you and derails your spirit as well as your plan?

Look to Nehemiah's example. When this happened to him, he prayed, remained firm in his goal and beliefs, and cried out to God for help. He kept going. He never gave up. Yes, his work slowed. It was necessary to take precautions by setting some of the workers as guards to ward off potential attacks. He knew what he was doing was right and would succeed, as he was putting God first. He knew he had God's providential protection behind him. What a feeling this is! Have you ever experienced it? If you have not, step out in God's will and do his work. You will perceive his peaceful reassurance and know how good it is!

Often, what seem to be obstacles and hindrances to us are reminders that we are doing the correct thing. As we are told, legitimate kingdom work will always be opposed by the people and forces of this world. Simply because we are in his will and doing his work does not mean we are going to be unopposed or have an easily victorious path through the world. These barriers show us that we need to depend upon God rather than solely our own abilities.

When we feel God's pull upon our hearts, his call to us, we need to pattern Nehemiah's example. We should adopt the dream or calling, plan it, and go about it to the best of our abilities, as he did. He accomplished his goal, and with the wall completed, he and Israel had a grand celebration. Nevertheless, while he must have felt extremely satisfied with his triumph despite the difficult work—let alone the intimidation, discouragement, social issues, and politics—still he knew his work was not fully done.

When Nehemiah departs for Persia and then returns, the physical wall is intact, yet the community is in shambles theologically, ethically, and spiritually. Tobiah, a chief opposer of the work, has a room within the complex of the temple itself. The Levites are not being appropriately supported, so they are having to live on and work their own land to earn a living, thus reducing the quality of worship. Further, there is no respect for the Sabbath. And the people are intermarrying with pagans. In summary, Israel has reverted to what led to their recent exile. How soon they forgot!

While they constructed a strong physical wall, the flesh of the people, as always, was weak. Further effort was needed. Remember, therefore, if you are called, even if it seems you have completed your primary task, it can flounder later. You may become discouraged. Was yours a wasted effort? In God's eyes, no. Nehemiah in such circumstances said, "I did what God wanted." He did not allow himself to be excessively burdened or discouraged by the troubles. He instead released them to God and got himself some rest and peace. He gave his frustrations to God. He told God he was true and did what he humanly could to the best of his ability. Being able to say this gives one great peace.

We must be true and faithful, even if our efforts meet opposition, even if we find discouragement as things work against how we would prefer or had foreseen things to go. God will remember our efforts, and they will be crowned if true and if we obeyed our Lord's commands. That is what we have control over. We must release the rest. By doing so, we will obtain rest from our frustrations just as Nehemiah did.

***

In conclusion, realize that through the Lord, our labors will be completed as he sees fit. As did Nehemiah, we must remain wise, motivated, and patient. We must not cut corners but give our all, putting our optimal efforts into completion. We must continue ethically and appropriately doing what our God tells us needs to be done. If the work slows or even grinds to a halt, do not be frustrated! If we are doing the best we can in and through him, we can trust he will complete the task through his will, in his timing, and ultimately, for his glory!

XVII. Obedient and Unashamed Believers:
Noah and Abraham (Genesis)

I know several completely selfless families of missionaries. These are people who have given up the pleasures and comforts we enjoy daily here in the West for the extremes of foreign lands replete with poverty, discouragement, distrust, and even persecution from those they seek to help. These brave souls are amazing examples. They are modern-day versions of the biblical characters who heard God's call and affirmatively replied to his command. I know one family who spent two years in a primarily atheistic Asian country and had only one reported conversion to Christ. They questioned whether their expended efforts were in vain. However, the ramifications of this conversion, reaching over generations, even if solely one person now, will likely be exceedingly huge for God's kingdom. No matter what the result, our Lord is in control. We must give our efforts and the harvest that results to him.

How hard is it to step out in faith and obey when we are ashamed or fearful of scorn and derision, hatred, or even plain old embarrassment and ostracism? What if we were to step through such worries and fears in true faith and do what God and Jesus Christ are calling us to do? What blessings would we reap for ourselves and for others?

Let us consider two stalwartly obedient biblical characters out of the first book of the Bible: Noah and Abraham.

A) Noah

We first meet Noah in Genesis 6. We are told that he is a "righteous man, blameless among his contemporaries." We are also told that he "walked with God" (Gen. 6:9).

In Noah's time, as today, the earth is full of wickedness. It is so evil that God decides to destroy every living creature except for eight people: Noah, his wife, and his three sons and their wives. God also saves breeding pairs of all land creatures.

To enable their rescue, God instructs Noah to build an ark. He provides very specific instructions regarding materials, size, and overall design. God tells Noah he will bring a flood to destroy the earth. He has him gather the animals to be saved in breeding pairs and stock provision for their time upon the boat.

When the flood comes, Noah is six hundred years old (and we complain about being old once we hit our forties!), a clear example that age makes no difference in whom the Lord can use! The ground opens, and the rains fall from the sky for forty days and nights. The water lifts the ark, and it floats with its precious cargo. All other living things on dry land die. The water stays upon the earth for one hundred fifty days. Then the waters begin to recede.

After one hundred fifty days more, the ark comes to rest on Mount Ararat. It takes another three months before the mountaintops become visible. Then after forty days more, Noah releases a raven and a dove.

The dove finds no resting place, so it returns. Thus, Noah knows the entire surface of the earth is still flooded. He waits seven more days, then releases it again. This time, it returns with an olive leaf, evidence that the water is receding. Seven days later, he sends the dove out again, but it does not return. Approximately two to three months later, we are told that the earth is drying out. Noah has been sealed in God's ark for over a year—approximately thirteen to fourteen months per the Bible's chronology. Noah finally opens the ark and views dry ground.

God tells Noah to leave the ark with the living creatures and to be fruitful and multiply over the earth. Noah builds an altar to worship the Lord. As Noah sacrifices and worships, God promises never again to destroy every living thing. And he sends a rainbow as evidence of this covenant.

***

Stirring lessons and examples multiply in Noah's story. He is rescued by God because he is righteous, yet he is not sinless. As God states in Genesis 8:21, "man's inclination is evil from his youth." Nevertheless, Noah was a man who did his best to follow God. Therefore, God cared for him, even as the worldwide flood eliminated every living thing upon the earth besides Noah's family and the chosen creatures.

This is reassuring evidence of God's protection and providence for those who know him and strive to be as righteous as a human possibly can be. God does indeed oversee, provide for, and guide the ways of those who follow him. Always remember this!

A further lesson is the fact that, despite what likely seemed to be pure insanity in the eyes of his community (and perhaps even in the view of his family initially), Noah doggedly follows God's instructions perfectly, doing all that is asked. Surely Noah faced societal ridicule and criticism from his neighbors. Imagine building such a large eyesore in what was likely a dry desert region. Nevertheless, while we are not told the exact details, Noah completes the tasks set before him by his God. He obediently endures the jokes and the sarcasm that were undoubtedly present. He simply and steadily does what he is told: "Noah did everything as God commanded him" (Gen. 6:22 TLB).

Once inside the ark, closed in as the floodwaters surged, Noah's job was not done. Imagine the thirteen to fourteen months he endured sealed within a dimly lit space with so many other living creatures. Imagine living in such cramped quarters with no escape from the hard work, loud noise, and awful smells. Imagine the waste removal necessary. There was probably no place to take a shower, let alone wash up.

Noah's great patience is also exhibited. Certainly, he was a captive sailor: once shut into the ark, he was quite limited in his options. Yet we are told nothing of discouragement, frustration, nor fatigue—although certainly he experienced such. Similar obstacles occur in our daily lives as well. We must continue to stay the course as Noah did, follow the plan, and strive for the goal that God has laid out before us. His kingdom work will succeed. Why shouldn't it do so with our efforts assisting it?

Imagine Noah's satisfaction when he departed the ark into a brand-new, spanking-clean world. There was so much potential in front of him. I also presume Noah was a bit fearful of his holy God, and rightly so. Yet, besides all the physical blessings clearly in front of him, he had to have been reassured by God's promise that he would never enact such vengeance again; the Lord vowed to nevermore wrathfully destroy all living things via flooding.

A final thought I have here is this: how hard was it for Noah to not tell his neighbors of the impending doom they all faced? As they went along with their daily lives, Noah knew everyone around him was condemned to death. However, since God had not instructed him to invite anyone else upon the rescue ship, he remained quiet about what was coming. Even if he had warned them, it is doubtful they would have taken him seriously, this man they perceived as their local crazy, this shipbuilder. They certainly would not have believed he was a reliable weatherman!

Fortunately for us, we do not have the restriction of a numerical limit to those who can be saved. Like Noah, we know that many of the unsaved around us will continue as such throughout their entire lifetimes and be condemned to eternal judgment. And yes, as Christian trailblazers we certainly will face scorn, derision, ridicule, persecution, and the like, much as Noah did. Yet, we are not building ships in the desert. We are offering Jesus Christ as the rescue, as the ark that can carry any believing soul into eternal rescue in paradise with our God forever and ever. He is the ultimate and final rescue. Unfortunately, this world often sees him as a nonsensical and impractical myth or ideal, yet we must never tire of presenting Jesus as the Savior he truly is.

B) Abraham

Abraham arises shortly after Noah in the book of Genesis. He is of the lineage of Noah's son Shem. We here see God's call to another righteous man, one initially called Abram, as he dwells in Haran. God calls him from what appears to have been comfort and prosperity amongst his large family group. He tells Abram to promptly leave his land and family. He promises that he will guide Abram to a new land and make of him a great nation. God states that he will protect Abram and bless all peoples of the earth through him.

Abram travels with his wife, Sarai, and his nephew, Lot, as well as some possessions and other persons. As he passes through Canaan, God promises Abram this land for his descendants. Abram then journeys through Israel's Negev desert into Egypt.

Here, however, Abram first shows distrust and lack of faith. He concocts a scheme that he feels will keep him from being killed by the Egyptians. He fears they will kill him to take his beautiful wife for themselves. He decides to claim that Sarai is his sister. Abram is then given livestock, camels, and slaves as gifts as Pharaoh takes Sarai into his own house. However, God strikes the ruler's household with plagues, and Pharaoh learns Abram has lied to him. So, he evicts him from the land with all he has.

Abram is now much richer. He moves between the Negev and Bethel, and he and Lot split up to better accommodate their large herds. Lot selects the Jordan Valley while Abram heads to Canaan.

After their split, God promises Abram's offspring will be in the land forever and that they will be as numerous as the dust, that is, too numerous to be counted. Despite Abram's long life without children, Yahweh promises Abram a son. We are told that Abram believes the Lord and that God credits his faith as righteousness.

Nevertheless, we see Abram's human side emerge once more. He and Sarai become impatient awaiting their promised child. So, Sarai convinces him to lay with her slave, Hagar, who bears Abram's firstborn, Ishmael. Ishmael is born when Abram is eighty-six. Yet, because his birth was of man's scheming and not God's primary plan, dissension soon arises amongst the trio.

Hagar lords her motherhood over Sarai. She rubs her face in the embarrassment of being barren. Sarai blames Abram for her sadness and frustration. She likewise treats Hagar contemptuously. Abram washes his hands of the whole situation and tells Sarai to do whatever she wants with Hagar, who is treated so severely that she runs away. The angel of the Lord appears and tells Hagar to return and submit. He tells her that her child will also become a great nation but will live in conflict with everyone else.

A full thirteen years later, God appears to Abram again. He repeats his promise to multiply him greatly through his progeny so that he will become the father of many nations. Also, God changes Abram's name to Abraham. He reiterates his everlasting covenant with him and his descendants and again promises Canaan eternally to them. He commands that Abraham and his descendants circumcise all male children. And he changes Sarai's name to Sarah.

Despite Sarah's laugh in an exhibition of disbelief, God again mentions Abraham's pending son and gives him more to hang onto by giving him a name: Isaac. Isaac, God says, will be the child through which God is going to continue his everlasting covenant with Abraham.

The ability of Abraham, as a righteous man, to plead for something in line with God's wishes is also manifested as he, next, successfully pleads for God to spare Sodom from its intended destruction.

We then see once more Abraham's human nature and fearful heart in Genesis chapter twenty. This time, out of fear for his life, he tells Abimelech, king of Gerar, that Sarah is his sister, just as he did previously in Egypt. (At ninety years old, she must have been amazingly beautiful if Abraham is still trying to protect himself in such manner!) Abraham justifies himself with some loose logic. He implies that because Sarah is his half-sister, he did not really tell a major lie.

There is no mention of God being angered over this. Instead, God simply steps in and takes control of the situation before adverse consequences occur.

Next, the Lord appears to Sarah, and she conceives and bears Isaac. Abraham is one hundred years old when Isaac is born. As Isaac grows, Ishmael, the older son, mistreats him, so Hagar and Ishmael are sent away into the wilderness. Nevertheless, God cares for them and repeats his promise that he will also make of Ishmael a great nation.

Finally, after at least thirty-five years of faithfully following God and developing a firmly trusting relationship with Yahweh, Abraham is given the ultimate test. He is asked to take Isaac to Mount Moriah and sacrifice him there as a burnt offering to the Lord.

Scripture does not tell us what Abraham is thinking. Certainly, many thoughts, possible alternatives, and even doubts are going through his mind. Nevertheless, we are not told about any of these. Abraham dutifully takes Isaac to the assigned place. He collects wood. He builds the sacrificial altar. He binds his son and places him upon the kindling pile. Holding the knife, he is clearly going to follow through and slay his son in sacrifice. However, the angel of the Lord stops him, stating that Abraham has proven he fears God because he was not going to withhold his only son from him. A ram caught by its horns in the brush becomes the substituted sacrifice. God then reiterates his promise of blessing Abraham and making his descendants as numerous as the stars of the sky and the sand on the seashore. He again states how Abraham will bless all the nations of the earth through his offspring.

In his old age, after Sarah's death, Abraham continues to follow God's intended plan. He makes his managing servant swear that he will not allow Isaac to take a wife from the pagan Canaanites. Rather, he commands him to go back to Abraham's own land and family. The servant journeys to find Rebekah, Isaac's wife-to-be. Their union will lead to the birth of the next great Hebrew patriarch, Jacob. Abraham passes from his worldly life, then, at one hundred seventy-five years of age.

***

Consider the character of Abraham. Imagine what you would do if you were simply told to gather up a few things and leave immediately for an unfamiliar place where you know no one, have no friends or family, and risk losing everything. Indeed, you would have to leave behind everything you know and are familiar with: your friends and family as well as the majority of your possessions that you cannot carry, including your home.

Any one of us would question this. However, we are simply told that Abraham went and did as the Lord told him. This was an amazing demonstration of faith. I am certain that his wife questioned him repeatedly and sternly because this decision likely seemed highly unusual to her and to their family. She was probably worried that her husband had become demented!

Somehow, I have always had the impression that Abraham dragged a reluctant and complaining wife out of Haran with him. Perhaps I am wrong, but that is the perception I get from the story, especially given the character Sarah displays several times in Scripture.

Therefore, as an attempt to test my hypothesis, one summer day I told my ten-year-old daughter, Lexie "You have ten minutes. Fill this backpack with whatever you would like to take. We are leaving on foot and going to a place that we do not know yet. God has told us to do this. I'm not sure how far away it is. And we are not coming back!"

As expected, the protest started immediately, in multiples!

"What do you mean we're going somewhere? Where is it? You mean you don't even know where this place is! We are never coming back to this house? Where will we stay? What about Mama? Does she know we're doing this? I cannot fit all my stuffed animals in this backpack! Can I bring my music? What about food and water? A flashlight? This pack is heavy!"

Nevertheless, in ten minutes I had her lined up out front with our backpacks and walking shoes on. Favorite stuffed kitties named Tiny and Mouse peeked out of her pink pack, overflowing with toys, books, a few clothes, and some candy and flip-flops. I gave her a wooden walking stick that I had carefully chosen, and we headed off down the lane.

It was rather hot. She was grumpy. She begrudgingly stomped off down our gravel road, groaning the whole way. Besides general complaints of thirst and heat, she was very concerned and quite embarrassed, saying, "What if somebody sees us? How can we be doing this? Are you serious? This is crazy!"

Aha! I knew it! Surely a daughter is at least the equivalent of a wife in her opinion of such a fool's crusade. And I then realized that Abraham was indeed blessed not to have had any children when he undertook his journey!

***

Despite the great faith Abraham showed in initiating his sojourn, twice later in Genesis he demonstrates fear of others, rather than trust in God's providential protection. He lies to the Egyptians and to King Abimelech, telling each that Sarah is his sister rather than his wife. Here we see his human heart's traits as well, despite being a righteous man.

I know many people who have similar thoughts and actions, things that they are sorry for later and, sometimes, that they never get completely over. They carry these around like heavy chains and baggage, but they must learn to give these to the Lord. In the case of Abraham, God did not hold him accountable or consider him unrighteous because of these misdeeds and lies. Even though Abraham got himself into trouble in these dangerous territories by trying to save himself, God rescued him. With Hagar also, it is likely that he was talked into the intercourse needed for conception by Sarai, according to the scriptural record. Yet, in doing so, he attempted to achieve a son by his own means. And it appears he was relatively easy to convince. He later washed his hands regarding Hagar's treatment, when she and Sarah squabbled within their tent. Surely having two women with whom he had been intimate under the same canvas was a very difficult spot. The African Maasai have a much better policy. While they can be polygamous (I have met some with five or more wives), tribal rules in the *bomas* (enclosed villages) I am familiar with mandate that the husband own at least fifteen cows for each wife. Even more crucial, each wife is given a separate hut!

Of note, it is widely accepted that the lineage of Ishmael became the Middle Eastern Arabian nations. These would evolve into the Muslim tribes that have been a thorn in the side of the Jews as well as the Christians for millennia. Again, man's attempts to step in and force his own ill-conceived ends typically produce severe consequences.

***

As discussed above, it is likely that Abraham had doubts, misgivings, and a general whirlwind of thoughts going through his head when he was told to sacrifice his only son, the one promised by God. What could

God intend by having him do that? He had been a faithful and righteous man. He had striven to obey Yahweh. Why then was this necessary?

How unfair it must have seemed to Abraham! He had believed God when he declared Isaac to be the next generation through which Abraham's descendants would bless the nations and become too numerous to count. Did Abraham suspect that God would stay his hand at the last moment? Did he reason that God would give him another son or even bring a slain Isaac back to life?

While we cannot know for certain, these are thoughts anyone might have in his situation. What is important is that Abraham did not look for a way out. He did not delay. He did not make excuses. He did not whine or complain about what he was asked to do. He got right to the task God commanded he perform. He trusted the Lord. He committed to give up the possession he loved most. And through this faithful and selfless obedience, Abraham solidified his position in God's kingdom work. What a lesson that is for all of us!

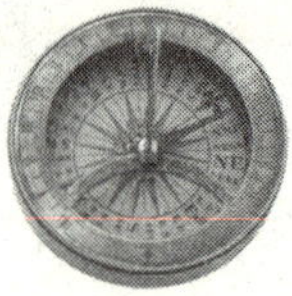

XVIII. "That Religious Person" (God's Trailblazer):

John the Baptist (Mt. 3:1-17; Mk 1:2-14; Lk. 1:13-17, 3:2-22; Jn. 1:6-8, 15-37)

John the Baptist—a man who possessed the spirit of Elijah—is an amazing example for us all. He was God's ultimate human trailblazer. Miraculously born to elderly parents Elizabeth and Zechariah, he spends his childhood in the wilderness. In adulthood he lives out by the Jordan River, a remote region of Galilee in Judea. There, he challenges the populace: rich and poor, powerful and common folk alike, including kings and religious leaders. He does not mince words. He calls some of them vipers and hypocrites. He urges all to repent of their sins. He proclaims that the long-awaited Messiah is soon to arrive.

John would not be swayed from his life's mission. He lives his entire life for God. He wears clothes of animal hides. He eats locusts and honey. He, by report, lives in a cave. He even calls out King Herod for his illicit union to his current wife, Herodias, who was previously his brother's spouse. John is imprisoned for this and later beheaded.

***

Throughout his life, John realized his role as the waymaker. He was the sole contemporary trailblazer for Jesus the Christ. His task was to make the way straight for the coming Savior of the world. Furthermore, he realized when his individual work was finished. When Jesus began his ministry, John said, "He must increase, but I must decrease." (John 3:30).

John simply did what he was supposed to do. And with such singleness of focus, he splendidly fulfilled his mission. Even Jesus was impressed, as he said, "In all humanity there is no one greater than John" (Luke 7:28 TLB).

***

- "There's that guy again, wearing that Jesus shirt."
- "Don't talk to me about that. I am not a religious person."
- "I can handle my own sin. I take full responsibility. I don't need any help or a Savior"
- "How dare you tell me that your Jesus is the only way?"
- "Who are you to tell me that I am lost?"
- "You Christians think you know everything!"
- "That is completely inappropriate to speak to me about God and Jesus. If you ever bring that up again, I will never come back to see you."
- "Stop talking about Jesus! If any of you religious fanatics come and burn down my house, I will know who to come after! Besides you, I have never spoken to anybody about this before."
- "I hate you Christians!"

These are all statements I have heard as I told others exactly what Jesus has done for us. I am certain you have heard many of these as well, if you have attempted to express your faith in him and spread his gospel of good news.

I continued to talk with most who initially made remarks like these. And if you, too, stayed in the game, how often have you also heard people make follow-up comments like:

- "I wish I had a faith like yours."
- "I used to have faith like you. I wish I could get it back."
- "I can see that there is something very different about you. Please tell me more."

These latter responses came from the exact same people who made the initial indignant exclamations. Nearly every single gospel conversation ends well in my experience if I remain humble and nonaggressive throughout and allow the Spirit to do his work. I can count on one hand the very few that ended poorly. The gospel is clear truth to all who will open-mindedly consider it. Therefore, let us consider the kingdom consequences were each of us a person like John the Baptist.

John had a job to do, and he was keenly aware of what it was. This rugged man devoted his entire existence upon this planet to its completion. He absolutely did not care what anyone else thought or said of him. Even from the time of childhood, he was noted to have been in the wilderness.

As an adult, he challenged the entire Jewish population, including the king and religious leaders, to repent and return to seeking the true God. He did not tone down his message because some of the Sanhedrin were there. He did not care if it offended persons who were foreigners or of other races or creeds.

John lived in a cave. He lived off the land, certainly not tasting any fancy dinner fare. He wore the clothes of a wilderness man as did the long hunters of centuries ago and as tribesmen still do in some countries today. His garments were functional. The animal skins kept him warm and dry. He did not focus upon splendid outfits, gourmet food, peanut M&M's, filtered drinks, lattes, or smoothies.

By minimizing distractions, he never strayed from his course. He kept his eyes always upon the prize throughout his existence. He started well, and he finished well. And because of this, Jesus pays him the ultimate compliment!

***

What would it take for us to alter our priorities, those things we spend so much time focusing upon, worrying about, and attempting to perform our best at? How could we, instead, develop the mindset of John the Baptist?

Start by imagining that your entire life goal is, first and foremost, to tell others about what God and Jesus have done. Your primary mission is to unabashedly proclaim the completed plan of salvation for all who believe in the sacrifice of Christ and will hand themselves and their sin burdens to him.

How radically would such an essential attitude change transform our relationships within our families and with our neighbors, friends, and work associates? What about within our own individual hearts and minds?

Yet, just how difficult would it be to do this? You may say, "Okay, but John was a bachelor. He had no children that we know of. God provided for his needs in terms of clothing, shelter, and appropriate food and water. And certainly, it was a different era."

Clearly, I understand that we have responsibilities to others: to our families and friends and to our work. We need to support our families, and as Christians, we are indeed to be present in the world. We cannot just give all of these up.

Nevertheless, despite these differences, can't we, in a manner similar to John, place in the forefront of our minds the goal of being certain that all with whom we associate have heard the gospel of our saving Lord Jesus?

In doing so, we truly become trailblazers to those around us. We are God's children. As his sons and daughters, we have work to do. We are his hands, feet, and mouth in this world.

And we all would love to spend time with a physical Jesus. How often do we say, "Boy, I'd really like to talk to the living Jesus of the Gospels for just a minute or two!"

Yet, Jesus has given us a way to do so. He has not removed himself from us. He is physically with and within us! Look at others to see Christ our Savior. And look in the mirror. Christ is in you, Christian!

We are the body of Christ. Yes, we are imperfect people, but God has used flawed people throughout history to bring about his kingdom.

Therefore, flawed as we are, we can change ourselves and our surroundings for the good. We can become more and more Christlike in this world through the process of our sanctification, as we are transformed into what God desires us to be.

Christianus alter Christus: the Christian is another Christ.

Conclusion

It was my first time to step foot on Chichagof Island in southeast Alaska, and I was with a reported master guide for brown bear. Unfortunately, if that were true, I was fully blind to his abilities even after twelve days with him. While mostly tales for another time, this was my first time in an autumn brown bear fishing stream. The creek was so chock-full of salmon you could barely take a step without treading upon fish. Bear sign was everywhere: huge tracks of the ten-to-eleven-foot monsters who dwelt there, fish remains, and prodigious scat piles. At dusk, a mist began to roll in. Rifles at our hips, we slowly advanced down the stream, watching, scenting, and listening.

The guide was first and I second, so I kept checking directly behind us. Suddenly, a huge brownie ran out of the dense rainforest foliage into the stream. A mere twenty yards behind me, he peered curiously at these two strangers in his territory, then ran back into the bushes. I tapped my guide on the shoulder and whispered, "Bear!"

He turned and looked but, seeing no bear, made a scoffing face. He turned forward and kept going. Sure enough, thirty seconds later, that same bear reemerged behind us, this time looking a bit more upset at the prospect of sharing his fishing hole with humans. He was clearly following us. Standing fully upright, the behemoth bruin eyed us and then lunged from the stream back into the woods. Yet, once more, my "bear, right behind us" whisper met with scorn and disbelief.

So, I grabbed the man's coat, spun him around, then made him stand in that salmon stream and watch our six o'clock. Ten seconds later, the big boy reappeared and again stood up. Here, however, we could circle into the wind, and as he got our scent, the bear seemed to lose interest. He lumbered off into the forest never to be seen again.

The outcome here could have been much worse. The importance of a capable, listening, and trusting guide cannot be overestimated.

***

Now, consider this scenario: It is a misty dusk. You are in distant mountains with no shelter nearby. Darkness approaches. Wolves begin howling. Storm clouds build above the timberline. Thunder rolls and lightning flashes above you. The driving winds usher in buckets of torrential rains. You are cold and wet. All around you is pure chaos. Spirits are failing. Control is waning. What must you do to step up and lead both yourself and your hiking party through these adversities to a safe haven?

We have each been given specific gifts by God, our loving Father. These are the abilities individuals can best employ for the Lord's kingdom purposes. When we activate these strengths and step forth with them in hand, we become his steadfast guides to others. We transform into his very own trailblazers.

We therefore need to discern the primary individual gift in each of us. We then must be certain we are using it to our fullest abilities. We must not minimize, deny, nor defer it. We all have major gifts as well as lesser skills. It, too, is a mistake to over-rely upon lesser talents while denying the greater.

What makes you feel most happy? What do you truly enjoy doing? Examining the answers to these questions will very often grant you a better understanding of your major gift.

Once you identify your talent, let our amazing Father's guiding Spirit awaken your thirst for his adventure. A life lived primarily for him will stir your heart, mind, and soul in ways you cannot yet imagine. You will assist your victorious Lord in his saving kingdom work. And you again become a guide for others. What else in our world of dark valleys, swamps, mountains, and thick jungles could be as satisfying?

***

All people need Christ as their trailblazer to complete the incredible journey laid out before them. When we grant him the role of our master guide, he leads and schools us in his ways. And this experience is what we transfer onto others as we attempt to lead them into God's kingdom.

But what exactly is this kingdom? Are we looking forward to only a heavenly realm? Is there an earthly component to Christ's kingdom? Is it visible to us in any form or manner in the here and now?

Besides the eternal, celestial paradise we have been promised after we depart this world, God's kingdom is among us now in daily life. Yet, we can only see it if we look for it. We must have, as Scripture states, eyes to see. If you can't visualize it yet, you need to pray for wisdom to be able to see it. Begin to look for it. It is pervasive in this world. It is holding back the onslaught of the darkness right now. And it has been doing so since the days of Jesus here upon the earth.

As Christ said, we, his people, are the world's light. So, don't miss it! His kingdom is here now! Our lives should be overflowing with kingdom purpose. We are to enlighten and season this world as his hands, his feet, and his mouth. We are to hold back the darkness by striving along with him.

The kingdom of heaven is not just something that we graduate into after death. Please, Lord, give us eyes to see and ears to hear, as well as minds to appropriately perceive this concept today. Let us recognize you in this world's goodness and light. Such assure us that we are not alone here as we play our part in holding back the shadows, while deferring and destroying the sieges and citadels of Satan!

***

What is God calling you to do? What is he asking you to step out and accomplish for him and his kingdom? What task has he placed in your heart and mind?

Sometimes, we just know—that neighbor we've been meaning to speak to, our Muslim or Hindu friend, that unsaved coworker, or that foreign mission trip or prison ministry we have been pondering. Such have been on our hearts and minds. God continues in his still small voice to remind us, to prick our consciences, if we will only listen and admit so.

Other times, we may feel completely unsure of where to next go or what to next do. In such cases, what should be our trail marker, our path discerner?

First, make time to get out into your quiet space, your wilderness. Forcefully blaze your way into it, if need be, perhaps by reducing your screen, internet, TV, sporting, and leisure activities. Turn off the cell phone. Clear your mind of all the crazy ongoing issues, worries, and conflicts even if just for five to ten minutes per day. Reserve that as a special time just for God.

Second, listen. Our Lord will speak to you if you put aside all those worldly distractions.

Third, meet and fellowship with him in your quiet time while asking what you should do. Commune with him in his word and in your prayers. Remember his promise: "'You will seek Me and find Me when you search for Me with all your heart. I will be found by you'—this is the LORD's declaration—'and I will restore your fortunes and gather you from all the nations'" (Jeremiah 29:13–14).

***

In conclusion here is a personal, individualized question: what is your percentage?

We all invest, I wager, a large percentage of our time in non-kingdom activities. We misspend excessive time on screens and technology. We expend great energies in our jobs and at worldly wealth creation and in needless anxiety and worry. Many overdo working out, sports, travel, or other leisure activities. And we often allocate excessive time to family, friends, and pets. This latter category can be tricky. We certainly need to devote significant quality time to our relationships. Yet, we must not overemphasize these to excess nor border on obsession.

Instead of pursuing these activities to excess, then, which kingdom actions deserve more of our time? The first would be allotting for more personal time with Christ. Here, we get to know him better through prayer as well as through the Bible as we study his Word. Relationships grow in direct proportion to the amount of effort expended. Do not shortchange this one in particular!

Second, strive for dedicated quality time with family and friends. Here, we employ our knowledge of who Christ is by leading, teaching, and displaying his example of a godly life.

A third category is church and related activities, including worship, Bible study, and small-group participation.

Fourth would be service activities like missions or other personal works outside the scope of routine church attendance. These include things such as kindness to prisoners, the impoverished, widows, the homeless, and orphans, as well as toward coworkers, friends, and other souls, be they lost or saved.

So, again I ask, "What is your percentage?"

We cannot let excesses of any non-kingdom entities rob us of our lives' greatest opportunities. Psalm 24:1 reminds us that everything we have been given (including our time and our free choice to spend it as we see fit) is actually God's! "The earth belongs to God! Everything in all the world is his!" (TLB). We and it are not our own. We are here for a far greater purpose than selfish endeavors and pleasures.

When you realize this fact, the question that follows is, "What do I need to reduce or perhaps even give up completely in order to optimally prioritize my time and my actions for Christ?" Now is our chance to know him better, to serve him, and to grow in him. We cannot let our times and opportunities pass us by!

Recognize that so much of what we do in our daily lives is inconsequential in God's divine plan for us and our world. Then, itemize a list of how you spend your time. Finally, ask which items need to be increased or decreased, and adjust those to enable a more positive kingdom outcome. Ask this question about each item on your list: "Will this really matter at my life's end or in eternity?" That one always floors me. It grounds me sufficiently well!

Therefore, we each need to formulate a personal vision. This is a kingdom plan for striding forward on our journey for the rest of our days. No two will be alike. But without consciously putting our minds toward the completion of this task, we will never achieve our optimally fulfilled states as Christ-like models and servants sent to this dark world.

***

I always like to ponder the circumstances of Luke 9:10. After Jesus commissioned his twelve men to go forth and proclaim the coming kingdom of God and to heal the sick and drive out demons, we are told: "When the apostles returned, they reported to Jesus all that they had done."

Can you even begin to imagine how joyous and excited those men were at that time? I strongly suspect their very cores resonated with a true joy and fulfillment no one can know outside of the work of our Lord. Imagine how proud Jesus was of his protégés, his assistant guides! While they clearly had much more to experience and to learn, they were well on their way. Christ's very own power within them was now propelling them ever forward!

Initially, Jesus was with them personally. And after ascending to heaven, he remained with them in the form of the Holy Spirit. That is how he abides with all today who are doing his kingdom work. Recall his words in Luke 10:19: "Look, I have given you the authority to trample on snakes and scorpions and over all the power of the enemy; nothing will ever harm you." And he will never renege on his promises.

We thus need to step out and do what we have been asked to do. Far too many Christians resist and defer any evangelizing. Common responses are, "That is just not my personality," or, "I am not forceful enough," or, "I am not capable of doing that, so I will let those more skilled people with missionary personalities do it."

One of my favorite statements that has been around for many a year is, God does not call the qualified, he qualifies the called. Look back through the pages of the Bible, including the multiple characters we reviewed. Were any of those people perfect candidates for God to use? Were any impeccable men or women without blemish, character flaw, anxiety, or worry? Don't you think they felt inadequate? Didn't we see their flaws many times, in every single case? Remember, these people were not exceptions. They were not supermen or superwomen of a type that no longer exists in this modern world. No, they are not exceptions. They are examples. Despite our radically different eras and cultures, they faced exactly what we face today. Nevertheless, despite their shortcomings, look at what God accomplished through them!

***

To succeed in our kingdom plans and goals, we need daily guidance from our heavenly Father. This alone will give us true direction in our lives. He is the perfect trailblazer, the optimal wilderness pathfinder for our journey through this world. Nevertheless, we need to be on the path that he has established for us. We cannot be set upon our own chosen course. Remember Psalm 119:105: "Your word is a lamp for my feet and a light on my path."

It is God's Word that allows us to find the optimal direction he would have us go. When we join with his guiding service, we will reach our objective as we step out and stand firmly for him and his kingdom plans.

Lord, we ask you now to show us what we need to do. Help us take the time to listen and discern. Reveal the plans you have chosen and the way that you would have us go. May your Spirit guide us on these paths, and may we never tarry long when we do venture off the Christian course.

Help us, Lord, to realize that true victory comes only when we yield our lives and desires to your plans. Success comes because we get your mighty power on our side. We need a solid fellowship with you, God, and with your Son, Jesus, in order to optimally achieve all the kingdom work you have planned for us. Contrary to the views of this world, we only become truly fulfilled in you, O Lord!

***

Whom can we always count on, absolutely and definitively, each and every time that we need him in this dark and crazy world of selfishness, corruption, protests, fearmongering, scammers, lack of responsibility, and general godlessness?

Consider Psalm 24:8: "Who is this King of glory? The LORD strong and mighty, the LORD mighty in battle" (KJV).

This mighty God is with us! Trust him. Step out in faith and do what he asks, even if you fear venturing into that unknown. Do it, and you will see how he helps you with your effort! He will be with you.

Always remember that our Lord is persistently with us and that he always instructs and supplies us with exactly what is required at each specific waypoint, be it words, deeds, or even simply waiting in some cases.

With God as our captain, as our master guide, we need not worry or feel inadequate. Oh, but we will, certainly. That is our human nature. Nevertheless, we need to trust him. Try this. Step out in faith to do something you typically would be very uncomfortable or resistant to doing. Visit a prison. Volunteer to help feed the line at the food kitchen.

Deliver Christmas baskets. Go on a domestic or foreign mission trip. Talk to a lost friend or neighbor. Try this just one time. I guarantee you will be humbled and blessed. You will also gain confidence and trust in the Lord and his abilities. The more often you do this, the more he builds your faith in him, progressively reducing your fearfulness and anxiety until these finally subside completely. There you reach the mountain's crest where, as these biblical characters did, you finally become fully confident. You then know for certain that you can do anything through God if you remain in him. He remains a loving Father to his children always. Do not fail him. He has a task for you to perform. Step out and do it in faith! You will not be disappointed!

***

We are God's children, his sons and daughters. He put us here as his warriors, his trailblazers. He strategically positions us on this world's battlefield to bear witness to him and his glory! Accept the challenge. Follow his path. His trail is the wise and the true passage. Jesus is our guide, our shepherd, our friend. Choose and stay upon the route that leads to light and to life. Yes, we make mistakes. Yes, we take missteps. We are human. Our feet will find some treacherous side trails. But he is ever with us and ready to forgive. Let us become who he has deemed us to be!

His plan far exceeds our petty, worldly goals. It is so much more than we could ever imagine for ourselves! Step out, take charge of your destiny, and do this in faith, Trailblazer! The world needs you!

Endnotes

1. Quotation attributed to Saint Ambrose, *De Virginitate*, 16, 199.
2. Augustine, *Confessions*, trans. Henry Chadwick (New York: OUP, 2009), 25.
3. The reason for evil in our world is a large topic and a worthy debate, albeit beyond the scope of this book. I do, however, devote an extensive chapter to this question in my prior book, *Rise and Soar*.